Engaging the Next Generation

A Guide for Genealogy Societies And Libraries

Copyright Information

Publisher: World War II Research and Writing Center, Woodridge, Illinois

Editor: Stephanie Pitcher Fishman
Cover Designer: Sarah Sucansky

Holik, Jennifer, 1973 –

    Engaging the Next Generation: A Guide for Genealogy Societies and Libraries / Jennifer Holik.

    ISBN 978-1-938226-62-5

This book is dedicated with love to
my three boys: Andrew, Luke, and Tyler Urban.
I'm very proud of you for taking an
interest in your family history.

Acknowledgments

This book could not have been written without the support of several people. I'd like to thank Andrew, Luke, and Tyler Urban, and my best friend Patti Fleck, for their love and support. The five of you are helping to make my dreams come true!

Thank you to my cousin Sarah Sucansky for designing my covers. Thank you to my good friends Stephanie Pitcher Fishman, for editing the book.

I would also like to thank Debra Dudek of the Fountaindale Public Library in Bolingbrook, IL, and Tony Kierna of the Schaumburg Township District Library, in Schaumburg, IL, for the many times they listened to me talk about the project and offered ideas and encouragement. If you have never attended one of their genealogy programs, you should.

How to Use this Book

This book was written with two goals in mind. First, to provide genealogy societies and libraries with the tools they need to build their own one-hour and half-day workshops. Second, to provide a complete set of lessons for use in additional genealogy classes or in the public or homeschool systems.

Part I – Workshops

Part I provides outlines which can be modified for different age groups. Each outline contains the least that could be discussed, written for 1st-3rd grade students. The speaking text provides the minimum amount that can be discussed with suggestions on how to modify it for 4th-8th grade students and high school students.

The appendices contain worksheets for the workshops, but these could also be used with Part II.

Part II – *Branching Out: Genealogy Lessons for 4th-8th Grade Students*

This section is meant to provide you with additional material to help design your youth programs or reach out to the schools. Should you choose to purchase the paperback copies of the lesson books to give each student in your program, your society can contact the author (jenniferholik@generationsbiz.com) about a bulk discount. The *Branching Out* books are available for 1st-3rd, 4th-8th, or high school students sold either as two books of fifteen lessons each or a combined thirty lesson book. See the Generations store for more information. http://generationsbiz.com/products.html

The 4th-8th grade genealogy lesson book was designed with the educator in mind, whether that educator is a librarian, leader, parent, or teacher. These lessons will guide students down the path of basic genealogy research. Lessons contain a goal, vocabulary, reading assignment, lesson, assignment, and some worksheets and projects.

Read through the lessons and reading assignments to ensure you understand the concepts. Then use the material as a guide to engage your students in their family history. Each chapter builds upon the previous chapters to help the student build their family history through basic charts, interviews, and records.

Table of Contents

Why and How to Engage the Next Generation

The Why

Family history is important for everyone. It gives us roots, helps shape our identities, and it helps us understand the past, present, and the future. As long as we continue to pass down our family stories, photographs, and traditions, we will stay grounded and understand who we are.

Genealogy societies and libraries should be engaging the next generation so our family history is passed down. We need to teach kids to understand and appreciate where they came from. If we do not engage the younger generation, our genealogy societies are destined to close shop because there will not be anyone to run them and pass on the information.

Understanding the past gives us roots. Those roots are important in an age when families move around a lot and live far from each other. Those roots are important when families are breaking up and later add step-parents and step-siblings. Each of those dynamics plays a role in who we are and helps define us and our family.

The How

One of the first things to consider when planning a genealogical program is the age group of the kids you will teach. First through third grade students require very basic concepts and hands-on activities to drive the point home. Older kids can handle more detail and less hands-on activities.

The second thing to consider is the goal. Is this class an introduction to genealogy? Is it an intermediate or continuing class? Are the kids Scout-type organization kids who are trying to earn a badge? Take the goal into account when planning both time and activities.

The third thing to consider is what kind of take away you want to give them. Should they walk away with a firm understanding of how to get started? Should your class handouts discuss only the class topics or should they also contain extra forms and resources? Should you give the students an assignment or project they complete at home just for fun or something they must do in class? What is the take away?

Engaging kids in genealogy requires creativity and the willingness to break things down into terms each age group can understand. For example, when you talk about a pedigree chart, you need to show an example of a completed chart. A project to help younger kids understand the concept might be to create a picture pedigree chart.

Another example is census records. When you discuss census records, maybe the 1st-3rd grade take away is simply that these records show us where our families lived at a certain point in time. For older kids, you can go more in depth and explain additional details that the census provides and what those details mean. High school kids should be able to analyze several years of census records and come to a conclusion about a family or issue.

Part I of this book is broken into two sections. The first section walks you through one-hour classes. One hour. Is that really enough time to teach kids the basics of genealogy research? Yes it is. When you create a one hour program for kids, you will hit the highlights of research and provide handouts with further resources.

The second section walks you through half-day classes. These classes have similar outlines and speaking notes as one-hour classes except they go more in depth and provide more activities.

Part II of this book contains all thirty lessons from the *Branching Out: Genealogy for 4th-8th Grade Students* books in their entirety. These lessons can be used as ideas on how to present materials or to create more challenging classes for youth.

Use this book to engage the next generation and help inspire kids to learn about their family history.

Part I

One-Hour Workshops

One-Hour Workshops for 1st – 3rd Grade Students

Tips

Parents should attend this program.

Encourage kids to bring information to the workshop.

Keep the concepts simple.

Use the suggested outline to build your program. Adjust as needed.

Create a PowerPoint presentation for the program with examples of actual documents.

Consider adding additional crafts.

After demonstrating how to complete the forms, allow some time for this activity.

Have all handouts in packets ready to present to each attendee.

Example Outline

1. What is genealogy and why should I care?
   a. Vocabulary
2. Should you believe everything you see and hear?
3. Why most people begin research
   a. They found some photographs
   b. They heard a story
4. Where to start
   a. Start with yourself
   b. Standard Pedigree Chart
   c. Optional Pedigree Chart
5. Activity – Pedigree Chart, Picture Pedigree
6. Family Group Sheet
   a. What it is and how to complete it
7. Activity – Family Group Sheet
8. Home Sources
   a. Vital records
   b. Photographs
   c. News articles
   d. Family Bibles
9. Activity – Be a Home Source Detective
10. Stories
11. Activity – Write a story with pictures

Workshop Preparation

Create folders with the forms and papers needed for each participant.
- Pedigree Chart
- Blank sheet of paper
- Family Group Sheet
- Home Source detective worksheet
- Story Page
- Additional worksheets:
  - What is Genealogy and Why Should I Care?
  - Home Source word search

Download Pedigree Charts and Family Group Sheets from any of the following websites. The other resource sheets are at the end of this book.

Ancestry.com   http://www.ancestry.com/trees/charts/ancchart.aspx

Family Tree Magazine

      Adoptive Pedigree Chart
      http://www.familytreemagazine.com/upload/images/PDF/adoptiontree.pdf

      Step-Parent Pedigree Chart
      http://www.familytreemagazine.com/upload/images/PDF/adoptiontree.pdf

Geneosity.com   http://www.geneosity.com/

Example Speaking Notes

Welcome to *[Insert Genealogy Group Name]'s* genealogy *program [replace genealogy program with your program name]*. Today we are going to talk about genealogy and how to document your family's history.

What is genealogy?

It is the study of one's family. It is tracing the lines of one's ancestors. Who are ancestors? Ancestors are those people in your family who lived before you. Tracing your genealogy is a little like being a detective. You have to locate the records and photographs that help tell the story and decide if those items are truthful.

Why should you care about your family's history?

Because it helps you understand a little more about yourself. It helps you understand more about why your family does some of the things it does and believes the things it does.

[Explain that Genealogy is about making connections. If a younger child is more comfortable creating the family tree of his step-parent or adoptive parents, let him do it. If a child wants to include their pets on a family group sheet or the optional pedigree chart, let them. They are making that connection that the pet is part of their family.]

Why should you start?

Many people, young and old, start their genealogy because of a project they completed for a class or because they heard a story. In some cases, people start because they want to know their family's health history.

[Tell a story about why you started researching. Even if it was for a class project, incorporate a story about an ancestor that made you curious.]

What did I do with all this information and these stories?

[The author stated: I started recording the information in my family tree charts and family group sheets. Then I started looking for records. Keep in mind you should never believe everything you see and hear. Find the records to prove the facts. You should modify this and explain how you started recording and saving the information.]

So let's get started on your family history. The place to begin is always with you. Write down what you know and work backwards.

Start with the pedigree chart. *[Explain how to fill this out and give the students time to complete some of it. Show them an example of a completed family tree in the PowerPoint or their handouts. Use a handwritten one or example from a genealogy program. Explain it is not necessary to know everything when you start. Fill in what you can.]*

Now let's look at another example of a pedigree chart. *[This chart was created by the author's first grade son, Tyler, in school when his teacher explained a family tree and making connections. The first graders really understood this concept. Draw this concept and include it in your PowerPoint Presentation and handouts.]*

© 2018 Jennifer Holik World War II Research & Writing Center

ACTIVITY – Work through Pedigree Charts

Option 1:
Ask attendees to go to the standard pedigree chart page of the handouts, and help them complete this.

Option 2:
Ask attendees to go to the blank page of the handout and draw the above chart for their family.

Give the kids a few minutes to begin filling out their pedigree charts.

Move to the Family Group Sheet. What is a family group sheet?

[Explain how to fill this out and give the students time to complete some of it. Show them an example of a completed family group sheet in the PowerPoint or their handouts. Use a handwritten one or example from a genealogy program. Explain it is not necessary to know everything when you start. Fill in what you can.]

ACTIVITY – Work through Family Group Sheets

Give the kids a few minutes to begin filling out their family group sheets.

Now that we have started with what we know, the next thing you should do is look at what home sources or documents you have in your home. You have a worksheet about home sources. Let's look at that. *[Discuss some of the home sources with the kids such as vital records, photographs, news articles, and family Bibles.]*

ACTIVITY – Be a Home Source Detective
[Explain the home source worksheet and encourage the kids and parents to explore these sources in their home.

Stories are an important part of genealogy. You can learn a lot about your family through the stories that are told. I'm going to tell you a story and then we can talk about the clues that might help me find more information. *[Tell a story that would interest the kids and ask them to tell you what they learned from the story about the person or family you were discussing.]*

ACTIVITY – Write a Story with Pictures

[Ask the kids to go to the story page in their folder and write a family story. It can be about anything: their pets, siblings, grandparents, a vacation, etc. The point of this activity is to make them think about the things they consider important, then they can write the story.]

Additional Project Ideas

Option 1: Create a Story about the Family

You will need:

> 12x12 scrapbook paper
> Crayons
> Pencils

Ask the kids to draw a picture of their family and tell a story.

Option 2: Create Picture Cards

You will need:

> 12x12 scrapbook paper cut into 3x4 rectangles
> Crayons
> Pencils

Ask the kids to draw a picture of a family member on one side of the card. Family members can include pets. The point of this activity is to help the child make a connection. On the back of the card they should write the name of the person or pet.

One-Hour Workshops for 4th – 8th Grade Students

Tips

Parent participation can be optional.

Encourage kids to bring some information.

Make the concepts more detailed than 1st-3rd grade.

Use the suggested outline to build your program. Adjust as needed.

Create a PowerPoint presentation for the program with examples of actual documents.

Have all handouts in packets ready to present to each attendee.

After demonstrating how to complete the forms, allow some time for this activity. The kids and parents can finish these at home.

Example Outline

1. What is genealogy and why should I care?
   a. Vocabulary
2. Should you believe everything you see and hear?
3. Why most people begin research
   a. They heard a story
   b. They found some photographs
   c. People are aging and want to leave something behind
4. Where to start (charts and forms)
   a. Start with yourself
   b. Pedigree Chart
   c. Family Group Sheet
5. Interviews
6. Home sources
   a. Vital records
   b. Photographs
   c. Letters, diaries, journals
   d. News articles
   e. Family Bibles
   f. Military records
   g. Church and cemetery records
7. Record examples
   a. Vital Records
   b. Immigration
   c. Naturalization
   d. Cemetery and church records
   e. Military records
   f. Newspapers
   g. Census records
8. Stories
   a. Activity – Write a story

Workshop Preparation

Create folders with the forms and papers needed for each participant.

- Pedigree Chart
- Blank sheet of paper
- Family Group Sheet
- Interview worksheet
- Home Source detective worksheet
- Story Page
- Additional worksheets:
  - What is Genealogy and Why Should I Care?
  - Home Source word search

Download Pedigree Charts and Family Group Sheets from any of the following websites. The other resource sheets are at the end of this book.

Ancestry.com   http://www.ancestry.com/trees/charts/ancchart.aspx

Family Tree Magazine

   Adoptive Pedigree Chart
   http://www.familytreemagazine.com/upload/images/PDF/adoptiontree.pdf

   Step-Parent Pedigree Chart
   http://www.familytreemagazine.com/upload/images/PDF/adoptiontree.pdf

Geneosity.com   http://www.geneosity.com/

Example Speaking Notes

Welcome to *[Insert Genealogy Group Name]'s* genealogy *program [replace genealogy program with your program name]*. We are here today to help you begin research your family history.

What is genealogy?

It is the study of one's family. It is tracing the lines of their ancestors. Who are ancestors? Ancestors are those in your family who lived before you. Tracing your genealogy is a little like being a detective. You have to locate the records and photographs that help tell the story and decide if those items are truthful.

Why should you care about your family history?

Because it helps you understand a little more about yourself. It helps you understand more about why your family does some of the things it does and believes the things it does.

Combining your family history with history in general gives you a bigger and more complete picture of your family. Using history, you place your family in the correct historical context. This means to look at their lives as if you were living in the same time period they were.

Why should you start?
Many people, young and old, start their genealogy because of a project they completed for a class or because they heard a story. In some cases, people start because they want to know their family's health history.

[Tell a story about why you started researching. Even if it was for a class project, incorporate a story about an ancestor that made you curious.]

What did I do with all this information and these stories?

[The author stated: I started recording the information in my family tree charts and family group sheets. Then I started looking for records. Keep in mind you should never believe everything you see and hear. Find the records to prove the facts. You should modify this and explain how you started recording and saving the information.]

So let's get started on your family history. The place to begin is always with you. Write down what you know and work backwards.

ACTIVITY – Work through Pedigree Charts

Ask attendees to go to the standard pedigree chart page of the handouts, and help them complete this.

[Explain how to fill this out and give the students time to complete some of it. Show them an example of a completed family tree in the PowerPoint or their handouts. Use a handwritten one or example from a genealogy program. Explain it is not necessary to know everything when you start. Fill in what you can.]

Move to the Family Group Sheet. What is a family group sheet?

ACTIVITY – Work through Family Group Sheets

Give the kids a few minutes to begin filling out their family group sheets.

Now that we have started with what we know, the next thing you should do is look at what home sources or documents you have in your home. You have a worksheet about home sources in your folder. Let's look at that. *[Discuss some of the home sources with the kids such as vital records, photographs, news articles and family Bibles.]*

[Move to interviews. Talk about why you should interview and how to get started.]

[Move to home sources.]

Now that we have started with what we know, the next thing you should do is look at what home sources or documents you have in your home. You have a worksheet about home sources. Let's look at that.

In genealogy, we need to prove the relationships between people through documentation. For the people listed in your tree, do you have birth, marriage, or death certificates? Do you have any wills? What about cemetery, obituary, or funeral records? Do you have a family Bible or baby books that list ancestors? It is important to note the source, or where you got the information, to prove the relationship.

ACTIVITY – Be a Home Source Detective

[Explain the home source worksheet and encourage the kids and parents to explore these sources in their home. Consider bringing some of your home sources to show as examples.]

[Move on to record examples.]

Let's look at examples of records. One thing to keep in mind when looking for records is the time period in which your ancestor lived. By putting them into historical context, you will learn more about their general life and learn which records were created in their lifetime. For example, today everyone has a birth certificate. But did you know that in Illinois they were not required until 1916? People did record the births of their children prior to this but not always. It just wasn't required. If a record was not required to be created you may not find some information.

[Provide examples of various records in your PowerPoint presentation. Include records that are specific to your state, when possible, to show the types of records available where you live. Consider putting examples of these records in the handouts.

Define each record type. Tell a story to go with each record if they are your personal records. By telling a story, the students become more engaged and interested.

Discuss where to locate the records you discuss. For example, vital records are held at X repository. Immigration records can be found on Ancestry.com, FamilySearch.org, and other places and repositories.

Discuss how to use each record type. Tell the students what specific information each contains. Explain any discrepancies such as census data changing for individuals every 10 years. One birth year you find in the 1870 census may be different in the 1880 census and so forth.]

a. Birth, Marriage, and Death Records
b. Immigration Records
c. Cemetery records
d. Military Records
e. United State Census Records.

[Next, bring the presentation to a close.]

Stories are an important part of genealogy. You can learn a lot about your family through the stories that are told. I'm going to tell you a story and then we can talk about the clues that might help me find more information. *[Tell a story that would interest the kids and ask them to tell you what they learned from the story about the person or family you were discussing.]*

ACTIVITY – Write a Story

Additional Project Ideas

Option 1: Create a Story about Your Family

You will need:

> 12x12 scrapbook paper
> Crayons, markers, or colored pencils
> Pencils or pens

Ask the kids to draw a picture of their family and write a story to go with the picture.

One-Hour Workshops for High School Students

Tips

Parent participation can be optional.

Encourage kids to bring some information with them so they can begin to complete forms.

Use the suggested outline to build your program. Adjust as needed.

Create a PowerPoint presentation for the program. Provide examples of actual documents in the presentation. Provide more examples than the 1st or 4th grade workshops.

Consider showing examples online if computers are available.

Have all handouts in packets ready to present to each attendee.

Example Outline

1. What is genealogy and why should I care?
2. Should you believe everything you see and hear?
3. Why most people begin research
    a. They heard a story
    b. They found some photographs
    c. People are aging and want to leave something behind
4. Where to start (charts and forms)
    a. Start with yourself
    b. Pedigree Chart
    c. Family Group Sheet
5. A note about sources
    a. Importance of citing sources
    b. Basic examples of citing sources
6. Interviews
7. Home sources
    a. Vital records
    b. Photographs
    c. Letters, diaries, journals
    d. News articles
    e. Family Bibles
    f. Military records
    g. Church and cemetery records
8. Record examples
    a. Vital Records
    b. Immigration
    c. Naturalization
    d. Cemetery and church records
    e. Military records
    f. Newspapers
    g. Census records
9. Project suggestions
    a. Stories

Workshop Preparation

Create folders with the forms and papers needed for each participant.

- Pedigree Chart
- Blank sheet of paper
- Family Group Sheet
- Interview worksheet
- Home Source detective worksheet
- Story Page
- Additional worksheets:
    - What is Genealogy and Why Should I Care?
    - Home Source word search

Download Pedigree Charts and Family Group Sheets from any of the following websites. The other resource sheets are at the end of this book.

Ancestry.com   http://www.ancestry.com/trees/charts/ancchart.aspx

Family Tree Magazine

   Adoptive Pedigree Chart
   http://www.familytreemagazine.com/upload/images/PDF/adoptiontree.pdf

   Step-Parent Pedigree Chart
   http://www.familytreemagazine.com/upload/images/PDF/adoptiontree.pdf

Geneosity.com   http://www.geneosity.com/

Example Speaking Notes

Welcome to *[Insert Genealogy Group Name]*'s genealogy *program [replace genealogy program with your program name]*. We are here today to help you begin research your family history.

What is genealogy?

It is the study of one's family. It is tracing the lines of their ancestors. Who are ancestors? Ancestors are those in your family who lived before you. Tracing your genealogy is a little like being a detective. You have to locate the records and photographs that help tell the story and decide if those items are truthful.

Why should you care about your family history?

Because it helps you understand a little more about yourself. It helps you understand more about why your family does some of the things it does and believes the things it does.

Putting your family into historical context, or looking at their lives through the time period in which they lived, gives you a bigger and more complete picture of your family. Placing them in historical context also allows you to look for time-period specific records. *[Provide some examples of records one may find in each time period. Be specific about your state records also.]*

Why should you start?

Many people, young and old, start their genealogy because of a project they completed for a class or because they heard a story. In some cases, people start because they want to know their family's health history.

[Tell a story about why you started researching. Even if it was for a class project, incorporate a story about an ancestor that made you curious.]

What did I do with all this information and these stories?

[The author stated: I started recording the information in my family tree charts and family group sheets. Then I started looking for records. Keep in mind you should never believe everything you see and hear. Find the records to prove the facts. You should modify this and explain how you started recording and saving the information.]

So let's get started on your family history. The place to begin is always with you. Write down what you know and work backwards. *[Discuss why this is important.]*

ACTIVITY – Work through Pedigree Charts

Ask attendees to go to the standard pedigree chart page of the handouts and help them complete this.

[Explain how to fill this out and give the students time to complete some of it. Show them an example of a completed family tree in the PowerPoint or their handouts. Use a handwritten one or example from a genealogy program. Explain it is not necessary to know everything when you start. Fill in what you can.]

Move to the Family Group Sheet. What is a family group sheet? *[Explain how the family group sheet differs from the pedigree chart. Explain its importance.]*

ACTIVITY – Work through Family Group Sheets

Give the kids a few minutes to begin filling out their family group sheets.

[Move to sources and citations.]

In genealogy, we need to prove the relationships between people through documentation. For the people listed in your tree, do you have birth, marriage, or death certificates? Do you have any wills? What about cemetery, obituary, or funeral records? Do you have a family Bible or baby books that list ancestors? It is important to note the source, or where you got the information, to prove the relationship.

[Explain what a source is. Explain what a citation is. Explain why it is important to cite a source with each fact, and give a brief example of how to do this for common citations – vital, books, websites, etc.]

[Move to interviews. Talk about why you should interview and how to get started. See the Appendix for an interview worksheet.]

[Move to home sources.]

Now that we have started with what we know, the next thing you should do is look at what home sources or documents you have in your home. You have a worksheet about home sources. Let's look at that.

[Discuss some of the home sources with the kids such as vital records, photographs, news articles and family Bibles. Show examples of home sources in the PowerPoint or display actual home sources.]

ACTIVITY – Be a Home Source Detective

[Explain the home source worksheet and encourage the kids to explore these sources in their home.]

[Move on to record examples.]

Let's look at examples of records. One thing to keep in mind when looking for records is the time period in which your ancestor lived. By putting them into historical context, you will learn more about their general life and learn which records were created in their lifetime. For example, today everyone has a birth certificate. But did you know that in Illinois they were not required until 1916? People did record the births of their children prior to this but not always. It just wasn't required. If a record was not required to be created you may not find some information.

[Provide examples of various records in your PowerPoint presentation. Include records that are specific to your state, when possible, to show the types of records available where you live. Consider putting examples of these records in the handout or have examples mounted on poster board around the room.

Define each record type. Tell a story to go with each record if they are your personal records. By telling a story, the students become more engaged and interested.

Discuss where to locate the records you discuss. For example, vital records are held at X repository. Immigration records can be found on Ancestry.com, FamilySearch.org, and list other places and repositories.

Discuss how to use each record type. Tell the students what specific information each contains. Explain any discrepancies such as census data changing for individuals every 10 years. One birth year you find in the 1870 census may be different in the 1880 census and so forth.]

    a. Birth, Marriage, and Death Records
    b. Immigration Records
    c. Naturalization Records
    d. Cemetery records
    e. Correspondence, diaries, old photographs
    f. Military Records
    g. Newspaper articles
    h. United State Census Records.

ACTIVITY – Write a Story

Stories are an important part of genealogy. You can learn a lot about your family through the stories that are told. I'm going to tell you a story and then we can talk about the clues that might help me find more information.

[Tell a story that would interest the kids and ask them to tell you what they learned from the story about the person or family you were discussing. Give the kids a story worksheet from the appendix and have them write a family story.]

Half-Day Workshops

.

Half-Day Workshops for 4th – 8th Grade Students

Tips

Parent participation can be optional.

Encourage kids to bring some information with them.

Create a PowerPoint presentation and use many examples of actual documents in the presentation, especially census to show how has it has changed over time.

Have all handouts in packets ready to present to each attendee.

Consider using online examples or have the students search for records themselves if computers are available.

Allow some time for the students to complete forms.

Example Outline

1. What is genealogy and why should I care?
   a. Vocabulary
2. Should you believe everything you see and hear?
3. Why most people begin research
   a. They heard a story
   b. They found some photographs
   c. People are aging and want to leave something behind
4. Where to start (charts and forms)
   a. Start with yourself
   b. Pedigree Chart
   c. Family Group Sheet
5. Interviews
   a. Why and how to interview
   b. Practice interviewing
6. A note about sources
   a. Importance of citing sources
   b. Basic examples of citing sources
7. Home sources
   a. Vital records
   b. Photographs
   c. Letters, diaries, journals
   d. News articles
   e. Family Bibles
   f. Military records
   g. Church and cemetery records
8. Hidden sources
   a. Artifacts
   b. Land records
   c. Licenses
   d. Medical records
   e. School records

9. Record examples
    a. Vital Records
    b. Immigration
    c. Naturalization
    d. Cemetery and church records
    e. Military records
    f. Census records
10. Project suggestions
    a. Stories
    b. Scavenger hunt

Workshop Preparation

Create folders with the forms and papers needed for each participant.

- Pedigree Chart
- Blank sheet of paper
- Family Group Sheets
- Family Interview Worksheet
- Student Interview Worksheet
- Home Source detective worksheet
- Hidden Source worksheet
- Story Page
- Additional worksheets:
    - What is Genealogy and Why Should I Care?
    - Home Source word search
    - Hidden Source word search

Download Pedigree Charts and Family Group Sheets from any of the following websites. The other resource sheets are at the end of this book.

Ancestry.com   http://www.ancestry.com/trees/charts/ancchart.aspx

Family Tree Magazine

    Adoptive Pedigree Chart
    http://www.familytreemagazine.com/upload/images/PDF/adoptiontree.pdf

    Step-Parent Pedigree Chart
    http://www.familytreemagazine.com/upload/images/PDF/adoptiontree.pdf

Geneosity.com   http://www.geneosity.com/

Example Speaking Notes

Welcome to *[Insert Genealogy Group Name]*'s genealogy *program [replace genealogy program with your program name]*. We are here today to help you begin research your family history.

[Ask attendees how many have done research prior to this class. Find out if they discovered anything they thought was amazing or cool. Discuss that.]

What is genealogy?

It is the study of one's family. It is tracing the lines of their ancestors. Who are ancestors? Ancestors are those in your family who lived before you. Tracing your genealogy is a little like being a detective. You have to locate the records and photographs that help tell the story and decide if those items are truthful.

Why should you care about your family history?

Because it helps you understand a little more about yourself. It helps you understand more about why your family does some of the things it does and believes some of the things it does.

Putting your family into historical context, or looking at their lives through the time period in which they lived, gives you a bigger and more complete picture of your family. Placing them in historical context also allows you to look for time-period specific records.

[Provide some examples of records one may find in each time period. Be specific about your state records also.]

Why should you start?

Many people, young and old, start their genealogy because of a project they completed for a class or because they heard a story. In some cases, people start because they want to know their family's health history.

[Tell a story about why you started researching. Even if it was for a class project, incorporate a story about an ancestor that made you curious.]

What did I do with all this information and these stories?

[The author stated: I started recording the information in my family tree charts and family group sheets. Then I started looking for records. Keep in mind you should never believe

everything you see and hear. Find the records to prove the facts. You should modify this and explain how you started recording and saving the information.*]*

So, let's get started on your family history. The place to begin is always with you. Write down what you know and work backwards. Discuss why this is important.

ACTIVITY – Work through Pedigree Charts

Ask attendees to go to the standard pedigree chart page of the handouts and help them complete this.

[Explain how to fill this out and give the students time to complete some of it. Show them an example of a completed family tree in the PowerPoint or their handouts. Use a handwritten one or example from a genealogy program. Explain it is not necessary to know everything when you start. Fill in what you can. Walk around the room and assist kids as they complete the charts.]

Move to the Family Group Sheet. What is a family group sheet? *[Explain how the family group sheet differs from the pedigree chart. Explain its importance.]*

ACTIVITY – Work through Family Group Sheets

[Explain how to fill this out and give the students time to complete some of it. Show them an example of a completed family group sheet in the PowerPoint or their handouts. Use a handwritten one or example from a genealogy program. Explain it is not necessary to know everything when you start. Fill in what you can. Walk around the room and assist kids as they complete the charts.]

Move to sources and citations.

In genealogy, we need to prove the relationships between people through documentation. For the people listed in your tree, do you have birth, marriage, or death certificates? Do you have any wills? What about cemetery, obituary, or funeral records? Do you have a family Bible or baby books that list ancestors? It is important to note the source, or where you got the information, to prove the relationship.

[Explain what a source is. Explain what a citation is. Explain why it is important to cite a source with each fact, and give a brief example of how to do this for common citations – vital, books, websites, etc. See the Appendix for a worksheet of examples.]

Move to interviews. *[Talk about why you should interview and how to get started. See the Appendix for an interview worksheet.]*

ACTIVITY – Have the Students Interview Each Other or the Program Presenters (15 minutes)

[Discuss the process. How did the kids feel about interviewing? Did they come up with any questions that were not on the worksheet?]

[Move to home sources.]

Now that we have started with what we know, the next thing you should do is look at what home sources or documents you have in your home. You have a worksheet about home sources. Let's look at that.

[Discuss some of the home sources with the kids such as vital records, photographs, news articles, and family Bibles. Show examples of home sources in the PowerPoint or display actual home sources.]

BREAK TIME – 15 minutes

Home Source and Hidden Source Detectives

ACTIVITY – Be a Home Source Detective

[Explain the home source worksheet and encourage the kids to explore these sources in their home.]

[Move on to hidden sources.]

[Explain the hidden source worksheet and encourage the kids to explore these sources in their home.]

ACTIVITY – Be a Hidden Source Detective

[Move on to record examples. Consider having computers available, if possible, to have the students locate records online. If that is not possible, have examples of records posted on poster board around the room.]

Let's look at examples of records. One thing to keep in mind when looking for records is the time period in which your ancestor lived. By putting them into historical context, you will learn more about their general life and learn which records were created in their lifetime. For example, today everyone has a birth certificate. But did you know that in Illinois they were not required until 1916? People did record the births of their children prior to this but not always. It just wasn't required. If a record was not required to be created you may not find some information.

[Provide examples of various records in your PowerPoint presentation. Include records that are specific to your state, when possible, to show the types of records available where you live. Consider putting examples of these records in the handouts.

Define each record type. Tell a story to go with each record if they are your personal records. By telling a story, the students become more engaged and interested.

Discuss where to locate the records you discuss. For example, vital records are held at X repository. Immigration records can be found on Ancestry.com, FamilySearch.org, and list other places and repositories.

Discuss how to use each record type. Tell the students what specific information each contains. Explain any discrepancies such as census data changing for individuals every 10 years. One birth year you find in the 1870 may be different in the 1880 and so forth.]

    a. Birth, Marriage, and Death Records
    b. Immigration Records
    c. Naturalization Records
    d. Cemetery records
    e. Military Records
    f. United State Census Records.

[Consider creating a scavenger hunt based on the records you discuss. Number each record and then place the records around the room. Ask the kids look for the records and write the number of the record next to the name of the record as they find them. Your worksheet may say "Birth Certificate number _____" and your birth certificate hidden in the room might be record number 6.]

[Move to the final part of the workshop – stories.]

Stories are an important part of genealogy. You can learn a lot about your family through the stories that are told. I'm going to tell you a story and then we can talk about the clues that might help me find more information. *[Tell a story that would interest the kids and ask them to tell you what they learned from the story about the person or family you were discussing.]*

[Next, bring the presentation to a close. Encourage the students to write a story they have heard from their parents or grandparents. Ask them to list questions they have after writing the story. Ask them to list records where they might search for answers. Provide an

example by telling your own story as described below. Ask the students to tell you about the clues and how they might help you locate more information.]

ACTIVITY - Write a Story

[Give the kids the story worksheet from the appendix and have them write a story about their family.]

OPTIONAL ACTIVITY – Fact Scavenger Hunt

[See the worksheet for scavenger hunt in the appendix. Provide the kids with example copies of the records listed on the scavenger hunt form. Help them answer the questions. This is only one example of records you can use. Create your own scavenger hunt to help kids fully understand the facts that may help their research.]

Half-Day Workshops for High School Students

Tips

Parent participation can be optional.

Encourage kids to bring some information with them.

Make the concepts more detailed than 4th – 8th grade.

Use the suggested outline to build your program. Adjust as needed.

Create a PowerPoint presentation for the program. Provide examples of actual documents in the presentation.

Have all handouts in packets ready to present to each attendee.

After demonstrating how to complete the forms, allow some time for this activity.

1. What is genealogy and why should I care?
    a. Vocabulary
2. Should you believe everything you see and hear?
3. Why most people begin research
    a. They heard a story
    b. They found some photographs
    c. People are aging and want to leave something behind
4. Where to start (charts and forms)
    a. Start with yourself
    b. Pedigree Chart
    c. Family Group Sheet
5. A note about sources
    a. Importance of citing sources
    b. Basic examples of citing sources
6. Home sources
    a. Vital records
    b. Photographs
    c. Letters, diaries, journals
    d. News articles
    e. Family Bibles
    f. Military records
    g. Church and cemetery records
7. Hidden sources
    a. Artifacts
    b. Land records
    c. Licenses
    d. Medical records
    e. School records
8. Record examples
    a. Vital Records
    b. Immigration

      c. Naturalization

      d. Cemetery and church records

      e. Land records

      f. Military records

      g. Newspapers

      h. Census records

9. Timelines

10. Organization of materials

      a. Digital files

      b. Paper files

11. Project suggestions

      a. Stories

      b. Case Study

Workshop Preparation

Create folders with the forms and papers needed for each participant.

- Pedigree Chart
- Blank sheet of paper
- Family Group Sheet
- Family Interview Worksheet
- Student Interview Worksheet
- Home Source detective worksheet
- Hidden Source detective worksheet
- Story Page
- Additional worksheets:
  - What is Genealogy and Why Should I Care?
  - Home Source word search

Download Pedigree Charts and Family Group Sheets from any of the following websites. The other resource sheets are at the end of this book.

Ancestry.com   http://www.ancestry.com/trees/charts/ancchart.aspx

Family Tree Magazine

      Adoptive Pedigree Chart
      http://www.familytreemagazine.com/upload/images/PDF/adoptiontree.pdf

      Step-Parent Pedigree Chart
      http://www.familytreemagazine.com/upload/images/PDF/adoptiontree.pdf

Geneosity.com   http://www.geneosity.com/

Example Speaking Notes

Welcome to *[Insert Genealogy Group Name]*'s genealogy *program [replace genealogy program with your program name]*. We are here today to help you begin research your family history.

[Ask attendees how many have done research prior to this class. Find out if they discovered anything they thought was amazing or cool. Discuss that.]

What is genealogy?

It is the study of one's family. It is tracing the lines of their ancestors. Who are ancestors? Ancestors are those in your family who lived before you. Tracing your genealogy is a little like being a detective. You have to locate the records and photographs that help tell the story and decide if those items are truthful.

Why should you care about your family history?

Because it helps you understand a little more about yourself. It helps you understand more about why your family does some of the things it does and believes the things it does.

Putting your family into historical context, or looking at their lives through the time period in which they lived, gives you a bigger and more complete picture of your family. Placing them in historical context also allows you to look for time-period specific records.

[Provide some examples of records one may find in each time period. Be specific about your state records also.]

Why should you start?

Many people, young and old, start their genealogy because of a project they completed for a class or because they heard a story. In some cases, people start because they want to know their family's health history.

[Tell a story about why you started researching. Even if it was for a class project, incorporate a story about an ancestor that made you curious.]

What did I do with all this information and these stories?

[The author stated: I started recording the information in my family tree charts and family group sheets. Then I started looking for records. Keep in mind you should never believe

everything you see and hear. Find the records to prove the facts. You should modify this and explain how you started recording and saving the information.*]*

So let's get started on your family history. The place to begin is always with you. Write down what you know and work backwards. Discuss why this is important.

ACTIVITY – Work through Pedigree Charts

Ask attendees to go to the standard pedigree chart page of the handouts and help them complete this.

[Explain how to fill this out and give the students time to complete some of it. Show them an example of a completed family tree in the PowerPoint or their handouts. Use a handwritten one or example from a genealogy program. Explain it is not necessary to know everything when you start. Fill in what you can. Walk around the room and assist kids as they complete the charts.]

Move to the Family Group Sheet. What is a family group sheet? *[Explain how the family group sheet differs from the pedigree chart. Explain its importance.]*

ACTIVITY – Work through Family Group Sheets

[Explain how to fill this out and give the students time to complete some of it. Show them an example of a completed family group sheet in the PowerPoint or their handouts. Use a handwritten one or example from a genealogy program. Explain it is not necessary to know everything when you start. Fill in what you can. Walk around the room and assist kids as they complete the charts.]

Move to sources and citations.

In genealogy, we need to prove the relationships between people through documentation. For the people listed in your tree, do you have birth, marriage, or death certificates? Do you have any wills? What about cemetery, obituary, or funeral records? Do you have a family Bible or baby books that list ancestors? It is important to note the source, or where you got the information, to prove the relationship.

[Explain what a source is. Explain what a citation is. Explain why it is important to cite a source with each fact, and give a brief example of how to do this for common citations – vital, books, websites, etc. See the Appendix for a worksheet of examples.]

Move to interviews. *[Talk about why you should interview and how to get started. See the Appendix for an interview worksheet.]*

ACTIVITY – Have Students Interview Each Other or the Program Presenters

[Discuss the process. How did the kids feel about interviewing? Did they come up with any questions that were not on the worksheet?

[Move to home sources.]

Now that we have started with what we know, the next thing you should do is look at what home sources or documents you have in your home. You have a worksheet about home sources. Let's look at that.

[Discuss some of the home sources with the kids such as vital records, photographs, news articles and family Bibles. Show examples of home sources in the PowerPoint or display actual home sources.]

BREAK TIME – 15 minutes

Home Source and Hidden Source Detectives

ACTIVITY – Be a Home Source Detective

[Explain the home source worksheet and encourage the kids to explore these sources in their home.]

[Move on to hidden sources.]

[Explain the hidden source worksheet and encourage the kids to explore these sources in their home.]

ACTIVITY – Be a hidden source detective

[Move on to record examples. Consider having computers available, if possible, to have the students locate records online. If that is not possible, have examples of records posted on poster board around the room.]

Let's look at examples of records. One thing to keep in mind when looking for records is the time period in which your ancestor lived. By putting them into historical context, you will learn more about their general life and learn which records were created in their lifetime. For example, today everyone has a birth certificate. But did you know that in Illinois they were not required until 1916? People did record the births of their children prior to this but not always. It just wasn't required. If a record was not required to be created you may not find some information.

[Provide examples of various records in your PowerPoint presentation. Include records that are specific to your state, when possible, to show the types of records available where you live. Consider putting examples of these records in the handouts.

Define each record type. Tell a story to go with each record if they are your personal records. By telling a story, the students become more engaged and interested.

Discuss where to locate the records you discuss. For example, vital records are held at X repository. Immigration records can be found on Ancestry.com, FamilySearch.org, and list other places and repositories.

Discuss how to use each record type. Tell the students what specific information each contains. Explain any discrepancies such as census data changing for individuals every 10 years. One birth year you find in the 1870 census may be different in the 1880 census and so forth.]

    a. Birth, Marriage, and Death Records
    b. Immigration Records
    c. Naturalization Records
    d. Land Records
    e. Cemetery records
    f. Military Records
    g. Newspapers
    h. United State Census Records.

[Move to timeline. Explain what a timeline is and its importance. Refer to lesson 26 in section two on Timelines for guidance.]

ACTIVITY – Create a Timeline

[Create a timeline of a person's life using actual records. For example, show kids records for one individual in your family that they can analyze and pull details from to create that individual's timeline. Show vital records, census records, immigration records, and military records if possible.]

[Move to organization of materials.]

[Refer to Part II, Lesson 29, and pull information to discuss how to organize and care for digital and paper files. Add your own ideas on organization. Give specific examples of how you and other researchers organize and store your records.]

[Move to stories.]

Stories are an important part of genealogy. You can learn a lot about your family through the stories that are told. I'm going to tell you a story and then we can talk about the clues that might help me find more information. *[Tell a story that would interest the kids and ask them to tell you what they learned from the story about the person or family you were discussing.]*

ACTIVITY – Write a Story

[Give the kids the story worksheet from the appendix and have them write a story about their family.]

ACTIVITY – Case Study

[Bring the workshop to a close with a case study. Choose someone from your family on which you have a lot of documentation. Outline the process by which you started research on that individual. Show examples of records you used, how you recorded the information, where you looked for additional information, both in repositories and records, and provide an example of a biography on the individual.]

Part II

Branching Out: Genealogy for 4th-8th Grade Students

Lessons 1-30

Items Needed

Most lessons in this book will require the following supplies:
- Notebook
- Pen or pencil
- Three-ring binder

Required Books:

You may purchase these or obtain through your library.

Croom, Emily Anne. *The Genealogist's Companion and Sourcebook.* Cincinnati: Betterway Books, 2003.

Greenwood, Val D. *The Researcher's Guide to American Genealogy.* Baltimore: Genealogical Publishing Company, 2000.

Szucs, Loretto Dennis, and Luebking, Sandra Hargreaves, eds. *The Source A Guidebook to American Genealogy.* Provo: The Generations Network, 2006. *Note: This book can be found on Ancestry.com's Wiki in full text. URLs are noted in each lesson.

Additional Resources:

These books are not required for this course. They are just additional resources for the parents and teachers, should they like to further their genealogical education or provide other resources for their children. Most libraries have these books or you may purchase them.

Books:
Greene, Bob, Fulford, D.G. *To Our Children's Children.* New York: Doubleday, 1998.

Hart, Cynthia. *The Oral History Workshop.* New York: Workman Publishing Company, 2009.

Hatcher, Patricia Law. *Producing a Quality Family History.* Salt Lake City: Ancestry, Inc. 1996.

Mills, Elizabeth Shown. *Evidence Explained Citing History Sources from Artifacts to Cyberspace.* Baltimore: Genealogical Publishing Company, 2009.

Pfeiffer, Laura Szucs. *Hidden Sources Family History in Unlikely Places.* Orem: Ancestry Publishing, 2000.

Rose, Christine. *Courthouse Research for Family Historians*. San Jose: CR Publications, 2004.

Sturdevant, Katherine Scott. *Bringing Your Family History to Life Through Social History*. Cincinnati: Betterway Books, 2000. **This book is out of print but can be found through libraries and used book stores.

Websites:

Docs Teach
http://docsteach.org/ from the National Archives and Records Administration

This website will help you bring history to life. By registering for a free account on this site you can create your own history activities. These activities support the National History Standards.

FamilySearch.org
http://familysearch.org

This free website contains many Wiki's with information about cities, counties, states, records, and more. These resources can be found under "Learning."

Genealogy.com *How to Cite Sources* by John Wylie
http://www.genealogy.com/19_wylie.html

This article introduces people to citing sources and the basics of how to do it. This is a good option if you do not wish to purchase or pick up at your library the Elizabeth Shown Mills book listed in Additional Resources.

The In-Depth Genealogist
http://www.theindepthgenealogist.com/

A digital magazine resource for parents, teachers, genealogists, homeschoolers, genealogy societies and libraries. There are forums, a blog, newsletter, and coming soon – webinars and other learning opportunities.

Teachers
http://www.loc.gov/teachers/ from the Library of Congress

This site offers materials to teachers to effectively use primary sources. It also contains self-paced online professional development modules.

Teacher's Resources
http://www.archives.gov/education/ from the National Archives and Records Administration

This site provides lesson plans and activities, school tours, and activities, using primary sources and more.

World War II Research and Writing Center

http://wwiirwc.com

The author's website contains information for potential clients, a blog about resources, repositories, education, books, and more.

Lesson 1: What is Genealogy, and Why Should I Care?

Goal

Learn what genealogy is and why it is important while exploring some facts about your family.

Vocabulary

Ancestors: A person from whom one is descended.

Descendants: Those living after a person who are in a direct line such as a son or daughter, grandson or granddaughter, etc.

Genealogy: A study of the family. It identifies ancestors and their information.

Family History: The research of past events relating to a family or families, written in a narrative form.

Interpreter: Someone who describes history through various mediums such as programs, costumed characters or lectures.

Public History: Practicing history beyond a school environment in places such as historical museums or government agencies.

Social History: The study of the everyday lives of ordinary people.

Tradition: The handing down of statements, beliefs, legends, customs, information, etc., from generation to generation, especially by word of mouth or by practice.

Lesson

Children often begin learning about their family history at a young age through storytelling. Through the stories they hear about their ancestors (grandparents, great-grandparents, and so forth) children learn bits of social history such as the stories of how the family spent the holidays, the jobs they held, or the places in which they lived. These stories can lead children into the study of genealogy.

Genealogy is the study of the family. The information gathered contains names of ancestors and dates and places where major life events occurred. For some researchers, names and dates are sufficient. For other researchers who want to delve deeper, they seek additional details to create a **family history.**

Family history is the research of past events relating to a family or families, written in a narrative form. Combining these two ideas together allows researchers to compile a more complete history of their family moving beyond names and dates to include the stories of their lives.

Social history is the study of the everyday lives of ordinary people. Examining the more "mundane" details of life can add color to your family history narratives. It brings your ancestors to life. Knowing where we came from and the history of our family gives us roots. It helps us understand why we live where we live, eat what we eat, act the way we do, and have the **traditions** we do.

Where can you learn about social history in the time of your ancestors? Through **public history** events! Public history is practicing history beyond a school environment in places such as historical museums or government agencies. For example, the National Park Service provides public history programs in the form of Civil War Battles or Civil War Days. Historical societies may provide public history in the form of an interpreter dressed as a famous person from history who walks, talks, and lives that person during the program.

Attending a public history event may provide background information on an ancestor. While you may never know what their experience was in a particular time period or event such as a war, public history can give you a basic idea of what it *may* have been like for your ancestor.

Ancestors are people from whom one is descended. This means those people who came before us. You and your ancestors have stories that should be told. How they should be told is up to you. Through these lessons you will trace your family and create a tree or pedigree chart with your child. You might make a photo collage or scrapbook. You will write a short story about one of your ancestors. Regardless of how you tell the stories of you and your ancestors, they deserve to be told.

What stories have you heard about your family? Do you have a Civil War ancestor? Did your family come to North America on the *Mayflower*? Did they immigrate between the years 1880-1930 when the highest numbers of people came to the United States? Or, are your ancestors or immediate family new immigrants?

As you work through the lessons in this book encourage your child to be as creative as they want. Please keep in mind that some children do not live in a household where both biological parents reside. Perhaps one biological parent is now married to a step-parent. The point of these lessons is to make connections. While genealogy is the study of the bloodline, if a child identifies more with a step-parent as his or her father or mother, consider allowing them to place that person in their tree and search that line. The same idea pertains to adopted children who may not know their biological parents.

*Note: Most genealogical software programs allow for the inclusion of a step-parent and adopted child.

Assignment

Part I: Write a story you have heard about someone in your family. Below the story, write the questions that pop into your mind and note any clues you see that might lead you to more information about that person.

For example:

John Zajicek lived in Chicago in 1871 when the Great Chicago Fire broke out. The family story said he tried to save the dining room table during the fire.

What thoughts come to your mind when you hear that story? A few that came to the author's mind were:
- Didn't he have a family to save?
- Why did he choose to save the table?
- John was a tailor – one who made clothing. Was that where he did his tailoring work?

It will never be known if John tried to save the dining room table but a one important clue comes out of that story. John Zajicek was living in Chicago in 1871.

From that clue, various records could be searched such as census and city directories to determine where he lived and how old he was. Did he really have a family to save or was he unmarried and living at home with his parents? Was he a tailor working at home or did he work somewhere else? These are things to consider.

Part II: Write down some of your family's traditions. Discuss with your parents and grandparents where those traditions came from and why you continue to pass them down.

Lesson 2: Where Do I Start, and What Do I Need?

Goal

Complete a **pedigree chart**, also known as a family tree.

Vocabulary

Maiden Name: A woman's surname, or last name, prior to marriage.

Maternal: Related through the mother's line.

Paternal: Related through the father's line.

Pedigree Chart: A chart outlining the ancestors of an individual.

Items Needed

Download and print the **Pedigree Chart** from Ancestry.
https://www.ancestry.com/cs/charts-and-forms

Lesson

Completing a **pedigree chart** or family tree is a visual way to see your ancestors and direct lines. It clearly identifies your parents, grandparents, great grandparents, and so forth. It is the first step in genealogy research.

The chart starts with one person and works backwards through that person's parents, grandparents, great grandparents, and so on. Write down as much information as you know. It is not necessary to have every detail at this point. Number the chart at the top right hand corner of the page with a number 1.

Begin with person number one to the far left of the page. Your child should write his name in this position and list his birth date and place as well. Next, go to person number two which is the child's father. Enter as much information as possible from his full name to the dates and places of birth, marriage, and death. Move to person number three which is the child's mother. List her information. Women should always be written with their **maiden name**. Their maiden name is the surname, or last name they were given at birth, prior to marriage.

Continue on to person four, who is the child's **paternal** grandfather. Person number five is the child's paternal grandmother. Add the **maternal** grandparents in spaces six and seven always putting the men on the top line of each family and the woman on the bottom line. Add as much information as possible to your pedigree chart.

If you have filled the chart and can continue farther back, simply put a number 2 in the box next to that ancestral line you want to continue where it says "Cont. on chart no." Then, print another pedigree chart and number that chart 2 in the top right hand corner. To add additional charts beyond that just continue to number the ancestral lines and new charts in the same fashion. Place your charts in your binder.

Example

Chart no. _____
No. 1 on this chart is the same as no. _____ on chart no. _____

16
b.
8 **Daniel Smith**   d.
b. 17 Sep 1913
p. Somewhere, Anywhere, Pennsylvania   17
m. 1933   b.
4 **Stephen John Smith**   p. Somewhere, Anywhere, Pennsylvania   d.
b. 4 Nov 1940   d. 14 Mar 1933
p. Atlanta, Somewhere, Ohio   p. Atlanta, Somewhere, Ohio   18
m. 14 Jun 1963   b.
p. Atlanta, Somewhere, Ohio   9 **Elizabeth Cantrell**   d.
d.   b. 3 Jan 1920
p.   p. Somewhere, Anywhere, Pennsylvania   19
2 **Daniel Smith**   d. 23 Apr 1930   b.
b. 24 Nov 1965   p. Somewhere, Anywhere, Pennsylvania   d.
p. Nowhere, Anywhere, Illinois
m. 22 Dec 1989   20
p. Nowhere, Anywhere, Illinois   b.
d.   d.
p.   10
                                                                 b.   21
5 **Amy Spencer**   p.   b.
b. 27 Jul 1941   m.   d.
p. Atlanta, Somewhere, Ohio   d.
d.   p.   22
p.   b.
                                                                 11   d.
1 **John Smith**   b.
b. 6 Jun 1991   p.   23
p. Nowhere, Anywhere, Illinois   d.   b.
m.   p.   d.
p.
d.   24
p.   b.
                                                                                       d.
sp.   12
                                                                 b.   25
6 **Thomas Jones**   p.   b.
b. 25 Dec 1933   m.   d.
p. Toontown, Disney, Florida   d.
m. 14 Feb 1964   p.   26
p. Toontown, Disney, Florida   b.
d.   13   d.
p.   b.
                                                                 p.   27
3 **Susan Lynn Jones**   d.   b.
b. 12 Aug 1965   p.   d.
p. Toontown, Disney, Florida
d.   28
p.   14   b.
                                                                 b.   d.
7 **Elizabeth Ruth Ashland**   p.   29
b. 19 Feb 1939   m.   b.
p. Toontown, Disney, Florida   p.   d.
d.   d.
p.   p.   30
                                                                                       b.
                                                                 15   d.
Prepared 16 December 2011 by :   b.
                                                                 p.   31
                                                                 d.   b.
                                                                 p.   d.

Optional Projects

Family Tree

Create a posterboard-sized family tree with photographs.

Supplies:
White posterboard
2 pieces of 12x12 black scrapbook paper
5 pieces of 12x12 green scrapbook paper
1 piece of 12x12 brown scrapbook paper
2 pieces of 12x12 cream scrapbook paper
2x2 photographs of you, your parents, your grandparents, and great-grandparents.

Note: It is ok if you do not have a photograph for each of these individuals. These photos could be themed – baby photos, wedding photos, etc. Or, just use whatever the child thinks is a great photo.

Adhesive such as scrapbook tape runner, glue stick, or bottle of white glue
Scissors, plain and decorative   Dinner plate
Pencil   Pen

Step 1:

Cut 15 – 2 ½" x 2 ½" squares out of the black paper. Set aside when done. Cut 15 – 2 ½" x 1 ½" cream colored rectangles. Set aside when done.

Step 2:

Print photographs and cut them out. They will look like small squares.

Step 3:

Glue or tape the photos onto the black squares you just cut.

Step 4:

Using the dinner plate as a guide, take a sheet of green scrapbook paper and draw a large circle in the middle of the paper. Cut out the circle. Repeat with the other four pieces of paper.

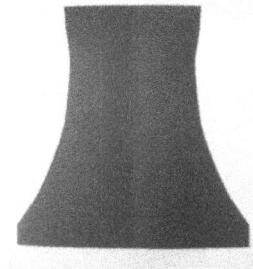

The circles can be cut out using plain straight-edged scissors or decorative scrapbooking scissors such as those with a wavy edge. These circles will create the green part of the tree.

Step 5:

Fold in the brown piece of paper in half. Draw an arc along one side. Cut along this line, and when you unfold the paper it will look like a thick hourglass-shaped tree trunk.

Step 6:

Glue or tape the tree trunk onto the poster board. Next, arrange three of the green paper circles across the top of the tree trunk layering them to overlap the edges. Add two more above them to create a huge green tree top. When you have the circles arranged the way you want, glue or tape them down.

Step 7:

Starting at the middle of the tree trunk, glue down the picture of yourself. Next, branch up and off your picture and add your parents. Glue these down.

Step 8:

Branch up and off your parents and glue down your grandparents. Continue by adding your great-grandparents.

Step 9:

Glue the cream-colored rectangles under each photograph and write the person's name, date of birth, and date of death.

Good job! Your tree is complete!

Additional Resources

Geneosity.com's Family Tree Forms
http://www.geneosity.com/category/genealogy-forms/family-tree-forms

Lesson 3: Genealogy Databases

Goal

Learn about the various genealogy databases available for researchers.

Lesson

Genealogists have many options when it comes to recording their family's information. Some prefer to use paper while others prefer to input the data into a genealogy database or an online family tree program.

The different databases and online family trees basically serve the same functions which are to:

- Record and display the family information in tree and group sheet formats
- Allow the input of facts and sources
- Provide the ability to add images
- Provide the ability to print reports and charts.

While the basic functions are the same, each program has its own pros and cons. It is up to the researcher's tastes and budget as to which program will best suit their needs.

Explore these database options on your own before presenting them to your child. Helping a young child enter information into a family tree allows them to develop organizational skills, attention to detail, and computer skills. If you choose to go with Myheritage.com or another source that allows sharing, consider sharing the tree with family so they can see what your child has accomplished. Those individuals may also be able to provide new information and photographs which may help further your child's research or which will encourage your child to continue learning about their family, etc.

Assignment

Read about the main genealogy databases available. Evaluate each and consider which would be best for your needs.

Myheritage.com

http://myheritage.com

This site offers a free option to create a family tree which can be shared with others or remain private. For added benefits you have the option to purchase a subscription.

Ancestry.com

http://ancestry.com

This is a subscription-based site that offers a free two-week trial period. You can create family trees on this site and also search for many records. If you only sign up for a free two-week trial be sure to download all the documents you locate and note the source. Most libraries offer a free version of this for in-library use.

Family Tree Maker

http://www.familytreemaker.com/

This is a piece of software created by Ancestry.com to create a genealogy database, track research, attach documents and sources, and run reports.

Legacy Family Tree

http://www.legacyfamilytree.com/

This is a piece of software created to create a genealogy database, track research, attach documents and sources, and run reports.

RootsMagic

http://www.rootsmagic.com/

This is a piece of software created to create a genealogy database, track research, attach documents and sources, and run reports.

Project

Create a family tree on Myheritage.com. Begin by completing the form on the main page and clicking **GO.**

Work through the site as you add the details you have uncovered to your family tree. Add as much detail as you wish.

Make sure you click on **Settings** and then **Privacy** to set your tree to the appropriate privacy settings for your family.

Lesson 4: The Family Group Sheet

Goal

Learn the purpose of a **family group sheet**. Complete family group sheets.

Vocabulary

Collateral Lines: A line of descent connecting persons who share a common ancestor. These individuals are related through an aunt, uncle, or cousin.

Family Group Sheet: A collection of names and facts about one family unit.

Items Needed

Family Group Sheets pages 1 and 2.

https://www.ancestry.com/cs/charts-and-forms

Lesson

The **family group sheet** is an important piece in your genealogical research. These sheets are where you list the family unit. One sheet is completed for each family listed on the pedigree chart as well as all other family groups (aunts, uncles, and cousins). Using these sheets, your child will record the names of each set of parents, all the children born to that union, and their vital information. It is important to search **collateral** ancestors because their records may yield clues about your main lines or the family as a whole.

Assignment

Now that your family tree or pedigree chart is complete, the next step is the family group sheet. The child should list the names of his parents in the top portion of the family group sheet where it has space for husband and wife. This portion of the chart applies whether a couple was married or not married. Please keep in mind it is ok for a child to list a step-parent or adoptive parents in these spaces. The point of this assignment is to make a connection and understand how to gather data on the family.

Next, add the vital information for each parent. Include the names of both the husband and wife's parents. Always remember to list women with their maiden names.

Below the husband and wife there is a space for the children of the family. The child should add himself and all siblings. The children should be listed in birth order.

A family group sheet should be completed for each family on your pedigree chart. If an ancestor was married multiple times and children were born of those unions, a separate sheet should be completed showing that family group. Store these forms in your binder.

Example

Father Daniel Smith			
Birth	24 Nov 1965	Nowhere, Anywhere, Illinois	
Death			
Burial			
Marriage	22 Dec 1989	Nowhere, Anywhere, Illinois	
Father	Stephen John Smith (1940-)		
Mother	Amy Spencer (1941-)		
Other spouse	Susan Lynn Jones (1965-)		
Marriage			

Mother Susan Lynn Jones			
Birth	12 Aug 1965	Toontown, Disney, Florida	
Death			
Burial			
Father	Thomas Jones (1938-)		
Mother	Elizabeth Ruth Ashland (1939-)		

Children

M	John Smith		
	Birth	6 Jun 1991	Nowhere, Anywhere, Illinois
	Death		
	Burial		
	Marriage		

F	Nancy Smith		
	Birth	4 Sep 1966	Toontown, Disney, Florida
	Death		
	Burial		
	Marriage		

Additional Resources

Ancestry.com's Family Group Sheet
http://c.mfcreative.com/pdf/trees/charts/famgrec.pdf

Geneosity.com's Family Group Sheets
http://www.geneosity.com/family-group-form/

Geneosity.com's Relationship Chart
http://www.geneosity.com/relationship-chart/

Review: Lessons 1 to 4

Vocabulary Review

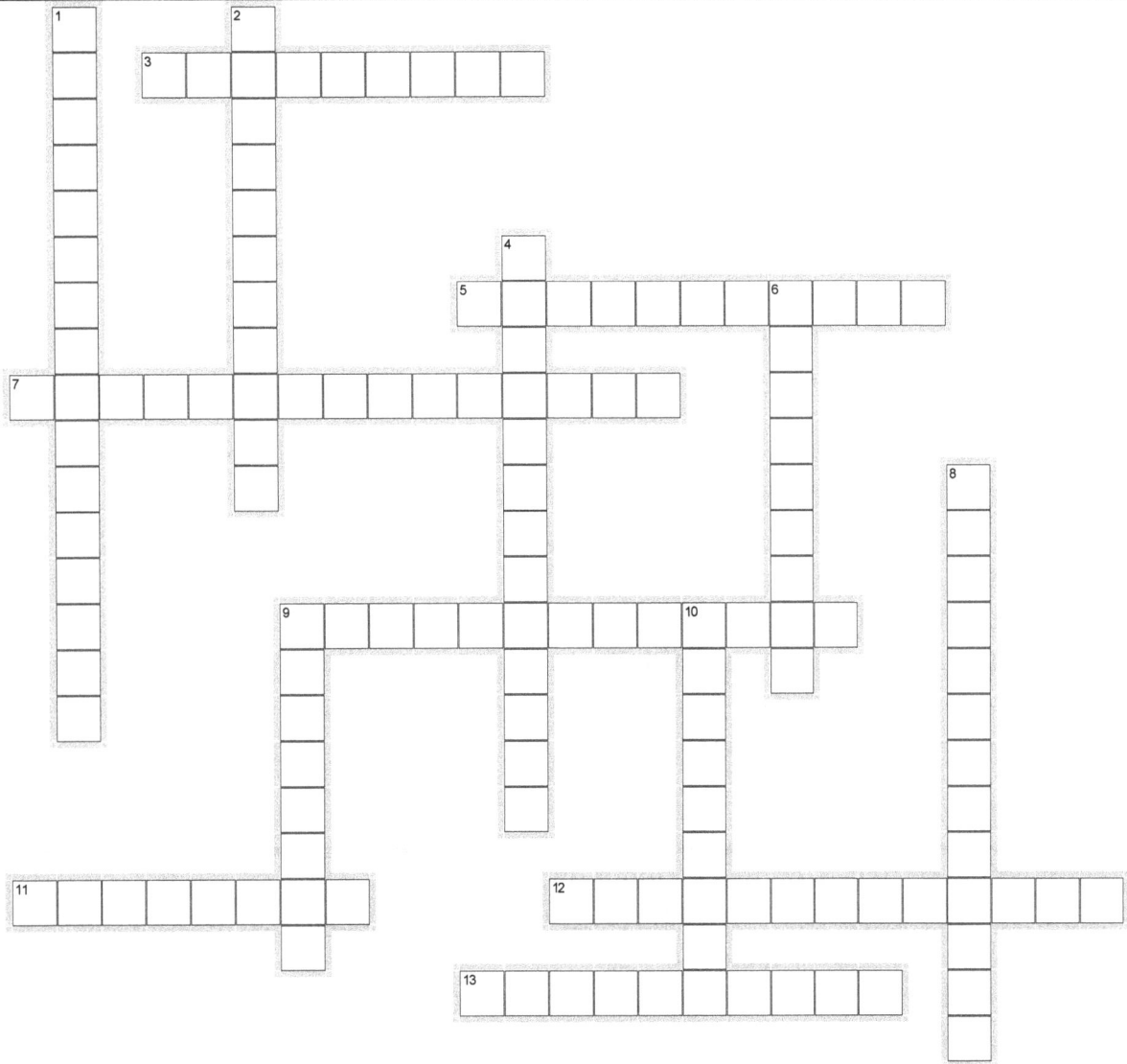

EclipseCrossword.com

© 2018 Jennifer Holik World War II Research & Writing Center

Word List

Ancestors   Collateral Lines   Descendants   Family Group Sheet   Family
History
Genealogy   Interpreter   Maiden Name   Maternal
        Paternal
Pedigree Chart   Public History   Social History

Across

3.   A study of the family. It identifies ancestors and their information.
5.   Those living after a person who are in a direct line such as a son or daughter, grandson or
        granddaughter, etc.
7.   A line of descent connecting persons who share a common ancestor. These
        individuals are related through an aunt, uncle, or cousin.
9.   Practicing history beyond a school environment in places such as historical
        museums or government agencies.
11.   Related through the mother's line.
12.   The research of past events relating to a family or families, written in a narrative
form.
13.   A woman's surname, or last name, prior to marriage.

Down

1.   A collection of names and facts about one family unit.
2.   Someone who describes history through various mediums such as programs,
        costumed characters, or lectures.
4.   A chart outlining the ancestors of an individual.
6.   A person from whom one is descended.
8.   The study of the everyday lives of ordinary people.
9.   Related through the father's line.
10.   The handing down of statements, beliefs, legends, customs, information, etc., from
        generation to generation, especially by word of mouth or by practice.

Lesson 5: Interviewing

Goal

Create a list of questions so you can learn more about your relatives. Learn how to conduct interviews.

Reading Assignment

Biography Assistant on Genealogy.com's website. Browse the "person" categories provided.
http://www.genealogy.com/bio/index.html

Research Tip 9: People as Sources for Family History by Raymond S. Wright III, Ph.D., AG
http://www.genealogy.com/tip9.html

Research Tip 10: Preparing to Interview a Witness by Raymond S. Wright III, Ph.D., AG
http://www.genealogy.com/tip10.html

Lesson

Interviewing relatives is a necessary part of genealogy research. For some, interviewing comes easy, while for others it is more difficult. Read the articles and discuss ways that you can help your child interview relatives. These could include:

- Helping your child write a letter to relatives which includes interview questions.
- Helping them create questions and interview someone in person or over the telephone.
- Helping your child video tape or record the interview if the speaker does not mind.

Field Trip

Visit your local library and look for interview books such as those listed in the additional resources section. Did you find any others that are helpful?

Assignment

Part I: Make a list of people to interview. Create a list of interview questions. Use the *Biography Assistant* suggestions from Genealogy.com as a guide to help your child add additional questions or discussion topics.

Part II: Interview relatives.

Part III: Discuss the new information gathered from the interviews.

Additional Resources

Greene, Bob, Fulford, D.G. *To Our Children's Children*. New York: Doubleday, 1998.

Hart, Cynthia. *The Oral History Workshop*. New York: Workman Publishing Company, 2009.

1. What is your full name?

2. When and where were you born? What city and state? What hospital?

3. Are you right or left-handed?

4. What is your eye color? Hair color? Do you wear glasses?

5. If your parents are married, when and where did they get married?

6. What is your job?

7. Do you have a nickname?

8. Growing up did you live in a house or apartment?

9. How much education did you receive? Where did you go to school?

10. What hobbies do you have? What hobbies did you have as a kid?

11. Did you get together with your family a lot while you were growing up?

12. Did you move a lot growing up?

13. What was your first car? When did you get your driver's license?

Add additional questions to this list. This should only be a guide to get you started. Write down the date of your interview and the address where you are living. Keeping a log of addresses when you take interviews or find documents can help you locate new information.

Lesson 6: Write a Story

Goal

Complete a brief story about the child's family based on information collected.

Reading Assignment

Review the *Biography Assistant* from Genealogy.com
http://www.genealogy.com/bio/index.html

Read *The Secret to Writing a Compelling Family History*
http://www.genealogy.com/74_sharon.html

Assignment

Practice creative writing by having your child collect all the charts and interviews together and write a story or multiple stories about the people in his family. Stories can be written about an individual or a family unit.

Each story should include a title, date, and author's name. Stories should include the information already discovered and recorded. Length does not matter.

Lesson 7: Evaluate the Information

Goal

Analyze and cite the information collected.

Lesson

Analyzing information is an important part of genealogical research. Helping your child (detective) re-examine prior findings can help them hone their detective skills. You can help by reviewing what has been written down. By looking again at the information collected your child can add new information to his pedigree chart or family group sheets. Did the detective catch all the details or was something missed? Did he write down a name and date only to discover after an interview that the date may be wrong?

Assignment

Turn your child into a detective! Revisit the family tree, family group sheets, and interviews you completed. Work through these forms and interviews with your child. Evaluate the information to see if anything new can be added to the family tree.

Lesson 8: Home Sources

Goal

Explore your home for sources that will add information to your family history.

Vocabulary

Historical Context: For family history, historical context is placing a person into a specific era or time period to view their lives and decisions based on the time in which they lived.

Home Source: A home source is any item or document that will provide facts on people in our family.

Interment: The location where a person will be laid to rest or buried.

Obituary: A notice of someone's death that usually contains a little biographical information about them.

Reading Assignment

Download the Home Source Checklist
http://www.bobcatsworld.com/genclass/Home%20Check%20list.pdf

Read this article so you have a clearer understanding of home sources. Use this to help in the discussion of what they are and what to look for in the home.

Lesson

Home sources are valuable to a genealogist. A **home source** is any item or document that will provide facts or clues about the people in your family. The checklist you printed contains many ideas for possible home sources. Let's look at a few of those in more detail.

Household Items

Family Bible

Examine your family's Bible to see if it contains the names and birth dates, marriage dates, and death dates of your ancestors. Note the name of the person who recorded the information in the Bible. Is this Bible something that has been passed down for several generations?

Family Photographs

Old photographs are a great place to start looking for information. Many times the names of the people are written on the back of the photograph or underneath if the photographs are in a scrapbook or album. Do your grandparents, aunts, or uncles have any that they would share?

Old Newspapers

Old newspaper articles can provide a wealth of information for a family history. Where can you find old newspapers? Check your attic, old books, photo albums, the family Bible, letters, and inside boxes of memorabilia.

What information can be found in an old newspaper?

- The military history of a family member.

- An **obituary** that lists the maiden name of a woman or the names of the deceased's siblings and children. An obituary is a notice of a person's death that usually contains a little biographical information about them. It also includes a notice of the funeral services and **interment**. Interment means where a person will be laid to rest or buried.

- World history information. Major events that occurred during your ancestor's life time. These details help put your ancestor into **historical context**. Historical context, for family history, is placing a person into a specific era or time period, to view their lives and decisions based on the time in which they lived.

School Records

Look for high school yearbooks which may contain activities in which your ancestors participated. Yearbooks are also a good source to use when proving the date and place of graduation.

Report cards are also a good source to track the school(s) attended by ancestors. It is also fun to look at their grades and compare them to yours. Did you and your mom or dad have similar grades in math or science? Or, are you a better student in those areas? This type of comparison shows the strengths and weaknesses we each have.

Search for artwork, school projects, and reports written by your ancestors. These items may not provide clues as to where the ancestor lived or specific details about their grades but help paint a picture of who they were at those stages in life. The author's mother wrote a lot of poetry in high school which she kept and passed down. Those poems would make a great compilation and show a side of the mother many probably did not know.

Military Records

Did anyone in your family serve in the Revolutionary War, Civil War, World War I or II, or other wars? You can search your house for:

- Service records
- Certificates or official discharge papers
- Pension files
- Draft cards
- Medals or patches from uniforms.

Each of these items will help build the military picture of an ancestor through pieces of information. One item will rarely tell the entire story.

Religious Items

Baptismal or Christening Certificates

Certificates issues upon baptism or christening will usually only contain the name of the church, your name, date of christening, possibly date of birth, and sometimes the names of the parents and godparents.

Mass Cards

Some mass cards or funeral cards may contain birth and death dates as well as burial location. Others may only contain the death date. Regardless, it is a good source of information.

Sunday School or Vacation Bible School Items

Many children participate in Sunday School or Vacation Bible School as they grow up. Do you have any church newsletters that discuss this and the achievements of the children participating? These items help build the religious story of an ancestor.

Vital Records

Baby Books

A baby book is technically not a vital record but it may contain copies of your birth certificate registered by the state or provided at the hospital. Baby books also contain other personal information about you in the form of height, weight, hair and eye color at birth, immunizations, and illnesses. Many times the book contains a record of the people who visited you in the hospital or provided gifts at a baby shower. Examine those names and addresses to see if you can identify other relatives.

Birth, Marriage, and Death Certificates

Birth, marriage, and death certificates are another good source of information. Details on certificates or licenses may include the names of the person's parents, the birth date and place, death date and place, an address, a spouse's name, and other information.

Make it Personal

Home sources do not only apply to our ancestors. They also apply to you!

Think about your own life. What home sources have your parents kept concerning you? Find out if your parents have any of the following and then examine those items.
- Baby book or scrapbook
- Report cards, school records, artwork, homework
- Religious certificates or church newsletters.

Assignment

Part I: Title a page in your notebook, **Home Sources**. Discuss the home sources listed in this lesson and the reading assignment. Compile a list of additional sources you can think of in addition to those listed.

Part II: Explore your home with your child and make a list of all the home sources you can find that were discussed in this lesson. Also include other sources of information you found during your search.

Part III: Review the home sources you discovered and add additional information to your pedigree chart and family group sheets.

Part IV: Write a one-page story about an ancestor or family using one or more of your home sources and world or local history events. Discuss how you think those events affected your ancestor.

Project: Create a Scrapbook

The purpose of this project is to help your child create a photo scrapbook of her relatives. Each page should note who is in the photograph. As you help your child create the book, talk about the people in the photographs so they become more real to the child. This is especially important if the people in the photographs are deceased or live far away. There is no required length. Let them be creative.

Optional: Decorate the pages and write a sentence about the person or photograph.

Project 1 (Younger Children):

Make 4x6 copies of family photographs that your child can use in their book. Cut pieces of construction paper into 8x12 pieces. Using a hole punch, create two holes on the left side of each piece. Tie the pieces together with string or yarn.

Create a cover for your scrapbook. Your child should include a title, their name, and the date. Encourage him to decorate the cover with drawings or stickers. Glue or tape one photograph to each page inside the book. The child should write who is in the photograph. If the date of the photograph is known, that should be recorded also. Decorate the pages as desired.

Project 2 (Older Children):

Make 4x6 copies of family photographs that you child can use in their book. Purchase a 12x12 scrapbook, colored paper and other decorations from a hobby or scrapbook store. Help your child create large pages that have multiple pictures on them. Label and date the photographs, and decorate the rest of the page as desired.

Additional Resources

Geneosity.com's Family Research Journal
http://www.geneosity.com/family-research-journal/

Geneosity.com's Research Source Record
http://www.geneosity.com/research-source-record/

Home Sources Word Search

```
U Q S Z N Y U H J S L B M I K
R Y D D L E O Y K U G I W N N
U J C I R M W E B E D B I T Y
J P M X E O P S N U S L V E M
J A I E Z N C E P F Q E Q R U
F Y D D N K A E A A A G E M G
Y R A T I L I M R E P W E E N
P H O T O G R A P H S E C N U
V Y L G C A R D S K Q D R T Y
V I Y P T P J S L A C Q U S P
C O T N J R E Y O W T H O R H
I C O A V J A Y O X Q N S Q H
X D B U L N C X Y U C Q U Q A
X G T E B H I S W S P L I R Z
R T E H M I X I D N S S A M H
```

BIBLE   CARDS   FAMILY   GENEALOGY   HOME
INTERMENT   MASS   MILITARY   NEWSPAPERS   PHOTOGRAPHS
RECORDS   SOURCE   VITAL

Lesson 9: Hidden Sources

Goal

Explore the hidden sources in your home.

Vocabulary

Artifacts: Memorabilia passed down through the generations.

Burial File: A file created on a military man or woman who dies while in service. This title was given to files created during World War I.

Hidden Source: A source of information you might not automatically think of when you search for family records.

Individual Deceased Personnel Files (IDPF): A file created on a military man or woman who dies while in service. This title was given to files created during World War II to the present day.

Memorabilia: Items collected and kept because of personal or historical significance.

Lesson

Hidden sources are things that are not automatically thought of when one begins genealogy research. The list of hidden sources in this lesson is by no means comprehensive. These are just some ideas to make you think about the items in your home that may contain pieces of genealogical data.

Household Items

Artifacts

Artifacts are memorabilia passed down through the generations. Artifacts usually contain a story and some clues about the ancestor who first owned the artifact.

Dictionaries and Other Books

The author discovered family names and dates on the back side of a torn off cover of a Webster's Dictionary from the 1950s. The author's grandmother had recorded the information here. Why it was recorded here is a mystery. Always check the inside of old books before getting rid of them.

Diaries and Journals

Ask your parents and grandparents, aunts, and uncles, if they kept a diary or journal. Diaries and journals may contain brief bits about a person's life.

Jewelry

Ask your mom and dad about special jewelry they have. Where did they get it? Why is it special to them? What is the story behind the piece? Is it something that is handed down through the generations?

Legal Records

Deeds

Deeds track the ownership of land or property as it passes from one person to the next. The county Record of Deeds Office typically holds these records, although the County Clerk has ownership in some counties. Deeds will list the names of the seller and buyer of property and will provide witness names and addresses. A legal description of the property will also be included which will help you locate the places where your ancestors owned land. Just because an ancestor owned land did not mean he lived on that land. Sometimes land was purchased as an investment or to use as additional farm land.

Probate Records

When a person dies, whether they had a will or not, a probate file may have been created through the court system. A probate record may contain the names and addresses of the heirs of the decedent, personal and real property information, a will, and final settlement details of the estate.

Medical Information

Medical Records

Medical records can be difficult to come by because of state and national laws regarding privacy. You may find some in your house. Look in baby books or immunization books that were kept for you or your parents. Also, check death certificates for the official cause of death.

Ask your parents about family illnesses. Did a certain disease run in your family? Was there a time when many people in the family died due to an epidemic? Record all of this information.

Midwife Records

Was your ancestor a midwife? Many midwives kept a log book of the babies they delivered, fees they charged and collected, and when the birth was registered with the county. Even if your ancestor was not a midwife, if those records can be found in the county in which your ancestor lived, it may provide additional proof as to the birth date of your ancestor.

Military Records

Body Transit Records

Did your family have someone who served in World War I, World War II, or beyond, and died during his service? Military men and women who died while in service to their country, abroad or state-side, have a file called a **Burial File** (World War I) or an **IDPF** (World War II and beyond.) Burial Files and IDPFs are files contain service information, serial number, next of kin information, interment and disinterment records, cause of death, and sometimes letters from the next of kin to the government.

Military Memorabilia

The author's grandfather joined the U.S. Naval Armed Guard during World War II. She has in her possession a Bluejacket's Manual dated 1940. This book is falling apart but contains all the information a sailor needed to know in 1940 and throughout World War II. This book contains the name of the author's grandfather along with his company, his dates of service, and the locations at which he trained. These types of details are excellent to add to your ancestor's military history.

Religious Records

Cemetery Records

Cemetery records may be lying around your home stuck in an old book or box. These records may include plot layouts that tell you who was buried in a specific area of the cemetery. These records help identify family members.

Make it Personal

Explore the history behind the artifacts you locate in your home. Did you find an old trunk? What was it used for and when was it used? Do you have an item that has been passed down through the generations? Is it something that relates to world or local events of the time period in which it originated in your family?

Think about the diaries, journals, and letters you may have discovered. Read them, and research the history of the time period in which they were written. Does the author discuss local or world events? How do they see things as compared to how you view them?

Assignment

Part I: Title a page in your notebook, **Hidden Sources**. Discuss the types of hidden sources listed in this lesson. Turn your child back into a detective and start searching for hidden sources. Explore your home making a list of all hidden sources you find.

Part II: Review the hidden sources located in your home. Discuss with your child what information was discovered. Add this information to your pedigree chart and family group sheets.

Part III: Write a one-page story about an ancestor or family using one or more of your hidden sources along with world or local history events. Attempt to use a home source in this story. Discuss how you think those events affected your ancestor.

Hidden Sources Word Search

```
V A Y T W O Y M Y B P A N Y Z
G D G V A R S G V D L L C R I
X P S G O I O Z B H B G E A L
O Y W T F L L R S R I S M N R
W B S U A A H I D D E N E O L
N I I E V V M V B T L Q T I A
H Y N T A R T I F A C T E T C
G E V Z U K Y R L J R B R C I
G B R Q I A E R Q Y W O Y I D
M T R B B C R Q L F A O M D E
R N T C O W W Y D E B K P E M
L A N R U O J I F O W S J U M
O Z D P Q M A C Z I A E V X P
M S R W Q R A P Y Z L G J J V
S G G Q Y C Y U S E D L K L J
```

ARTIFACT   BOOKS   CEMETERY   DIARY
DICTIONARY   FAMILY   GENEALOGY   HIDDEN
HISTORY   JEWELRY   JOURNAL   MEDICAL
MEMORABILIA   OBITUARY   RECORDS

Lesson 10: Primary Sources and Citations

Goal

Understand what a primary source is, where to find it, and its role in genealogy research. Learn the importance of source citations.

Vocabulary

Citation: Bibliographic origin of evidence.

Derivative Source: Material that is manipulated through copying such as extracts, transcriptions, abstracts, translations, and authored works.

Original Source: Material that has been unaltered and remains in its original form.

Primary Source: A piece of evidence from the past that was created during the event.

Source: People, documents, artifacts, and print or digital materials.

Item Needed

Library of Congress: Primary Source Analysis Tool
http://www.loc.gov/teachers/usingprimarysources/resources/Primary_Source_Analysis_Tool.pdf

National Archives Written Document Analysis Worksheet
http://www.archives.gov/education/lessons/worksheets/written_document_analysis_worksheet.pdf

Lesson

As your child gathers information in the form of photographs, documents, oral histories, home and hidden sources, it is important to help them understand the differences among source types. Primary sources, secondary sources, and evidence are difficult concepts for younger children but should be discussed. This is a good time to explain to your child that not everything they see or hear is the truth. This concept applies in many areas of life from what is seen on TV to what is on the internet or what someone tells us in conversation.

Primary sources are an asset to genealogists. A primary source is a piece of evidence from the past that was created during the event. They provide rich, though not always complete or correct, data. Humans make mistakes and even primary sources will contain spelling errors, incorrect dates, and information omissions.

Examples of primary sources:

- Diaries
- Letters
- Vital records
- Newspaper articles
- Court records and legal documents
- Probate records such as wills.

Primary sources can help family history come alive and should be "listened to" during the research process. Be wary, though, because not everything you read is the truth. Sometimes the truth is stretched to make an event more exciting. Various pieces of evidence should be consulted while examining a topic before drawing conclusions and writing your own piece based on the evidence.

Source citations are important when researching your family's history. When you locate records and add pieces of information into your genealogy you should note the source from which it came. Writing a source citation for the record or book from which you obtained the information allows you and others to recheck the source in the future. It also adds validity to your work. Source citations in genealogy should go beyond the basic facts of locating the source. They should also identify the type of source (website, book, document, etc.) so accurate analysis can be made.

Citing a source is an important concept for children as they progress through school. The more they write reports the more teachers will require them to say where they obtained their information. It helps them validate their facts.

Examples of Source Citations

Fact: Military service
Item: Photograph of Great-grandpa Joseph Holik in a World War II uniform

When you note the fact that Joseph served in World War II in your family group sheets or database, simply add that the information came from a photograph of him in uniform.

If you do not possess the photograph, also specifying who owns and possesses it will help you locate it in the future.

Example citation: Joseph Holik, ca 1943; photograph, privately held by Jennifer Holik [ADDRESS FOR PRIVATE USE] Woodridge, Illinois, 2012.

Discuss: What clues can you obtain from this photograph?

Fact: Birth or death date and place
Item: Birth certificate or death certificate

Your child will list these dates and places in the family tree and family group sheets. Simply add a source to the fact that says birth (or death) certificate, state of X, certificate number (usually found in the upper right corner), name of the person, and the year of the certificate.

Fact: Marriage
Item: Marriage certificate or photograph

Discuss: What clues can you obtain from this photograph?

Example citation: Frank Brouk and Anna Schubert, ca 1904; photograph, privately held by Jennifer Holik [ADDRESS FOR PRIVATE USE] Woodridge, Illinois, 2012.

Assignment

Part I: Analyze the documents you found in your home using the National Archives

Written Document Analysis Worksheet

http://www.archives.gov/education/lessons/worksheets/written_document_analysis_worksheet.pdf   Then extract primary information from your documents and add that information to your pedigree chart and family group sheets.

Part II: Cite your sources. Use the reading assignment to help you cite your sources on the documents you have located to this point in your research. Write your source citations on each document.

Additional Resources

Mills, Elizabeth Shown. *Evidence Explained Citing History Sources from Artifacts to Cyberspace.* Baltimore: Genealogical Publishing Company, 2009.

Library of Congress Teacher's Guide Resources

- Analyzing Primary Sources

http://www.loc.gov/teachers/usingprimarysources/resources/Analyzing_Primary_Sources.pdf

- Analyzing Books and Other Printed Sources

http://www.loc.gov/teachers/usingprimarysources/resources/Analyzing_Books_and_Other_Printed_Texts.pdf

- Finding Primary Sources

http://www.loc.gov/teachers/usingprimarysources/finding.html

Lesson 11: Secondary Sources

Goal

Understand and use secondary sources in genealogical research.

Vocabulary

Secondary Source: Sources created after an event by people who do not have firsthand knowledge of the event.

Item Needed

Learn more about Primary and Secondary Sources through University of MA – Boston.
https://umb.libguides.com/PrimarySources/secondary

Reading Assignment

Research Tip 12: Evaluating Written and Oral Evidence on Genealogy.com
http://www.genealogy.com/tip12.html

Lesson

Secondary sources are those created after an event by people who do not have firsthand knowledge of the event. An example of a secondary source is a newspaper or magazine article, documentary, or book written by people who studied primary sources. Another example of secondary sources is a birth or marriage date listed on a death certificate. The informant was likely not present at either event and therefore could not be the primary source for that information.

Secondary sources can lead researchers to new primary sources. They can also help researchers form an opinion of an event or person. These sources can help answer questions about a topic which will help a researcher narrow their focus or expand a story.

Secondary sources, like primary sources, are a difficult concept for younger children. Help them to understand the basic idea as you look at the records and items collected so far. The basic idea is that the person providing the information was not likely present when the event occurred.

Example

Item: Death certificate completed by the wife of the deceased

Fact: Birth date

The wife was not present at the birth of her husband therefore this is a secondary source of information.

Source: Chicago, Illinois, Death Certificate, certificate no. 22776, Alex Urban, Illinois State Archives, Springfield, IL.

Assignment

Examine the documents you have located so far. Document the secondary source information from these records in your family group sheets.

Additional Resources

Greenwood, Val D. *The Researcher's Guide to American Genealogy*. Baltimore: Genealogical Publishing Company, 2000. Read pages 68-72.

Mills, Elizabeth Shown. *Evidence Explained Citing History Sources from Artifacts to Cyberspace*. Baltimore: Genealogical Publishing Company, 2009. Read pages 23-26.

Lesson 12: Evidence, Fact and Proof

Goal

Understand what evidence, fact, and proof are and how they help your genealogical research.

Vocabulary

Direct Evidence: Information relevant to genealogy research that seems to answer a specific question.

Evidence: Something that pertains to an issue in question.

Fact: Something that actually exists; truth; reality.

Indirect Evidence: Information relevant to genealogy research that cannot answer a specific question without other evidence or records.

Proof: Evidence or argument establishing or helping to establish a fact or truth of a statement.

Reading Assignment

Greenwood, Val D. *The Researcher's Guide to American Genealogy.* Baltimore: Genealogical Publishing Company, 2000. Read chapter 4, pages 65-78.

Lesson

When you begin researching your genealogy you start by listing the **facts** you know. Sallie Smith is working on her genealogy she has the following facts: Grandpa Joe Smith was born July 8, 1902 in Chicago, Illinois. He married Wilma Davidson in 1923 in Chicago, Illinois. They had your father, Joseph Smith, in 1925.

Now, you need to prove these facts and find **evidence** that supports them. **Direct evidence** is information that answers a question pertaining to your research. Joe Smith was born in 1902. Direct evidence of this fact may be his birth certificate. The birth certificate lists the date he was born. **Indirect evidence** supporting the fact Joe Smith was born in 1902 may be a 1910 or 1920 census that provides his year of birth. The census may say 1902 but does not provide a full date.

Combining the evidence together makes **proof**. Your child can say with greater certainty that Joe Smith was born in 1902 because he has a birth certificate (evidence) and census record (evidence) to support his fact.

Assignment

The reading assignment is meant to give kids an idea of how evidence, fact, and proof work. Discuss these concepts with your child to make sure they have a general idea of how these pieces fit together. These will be important concepts to understand as you work through the various record types and assignments.

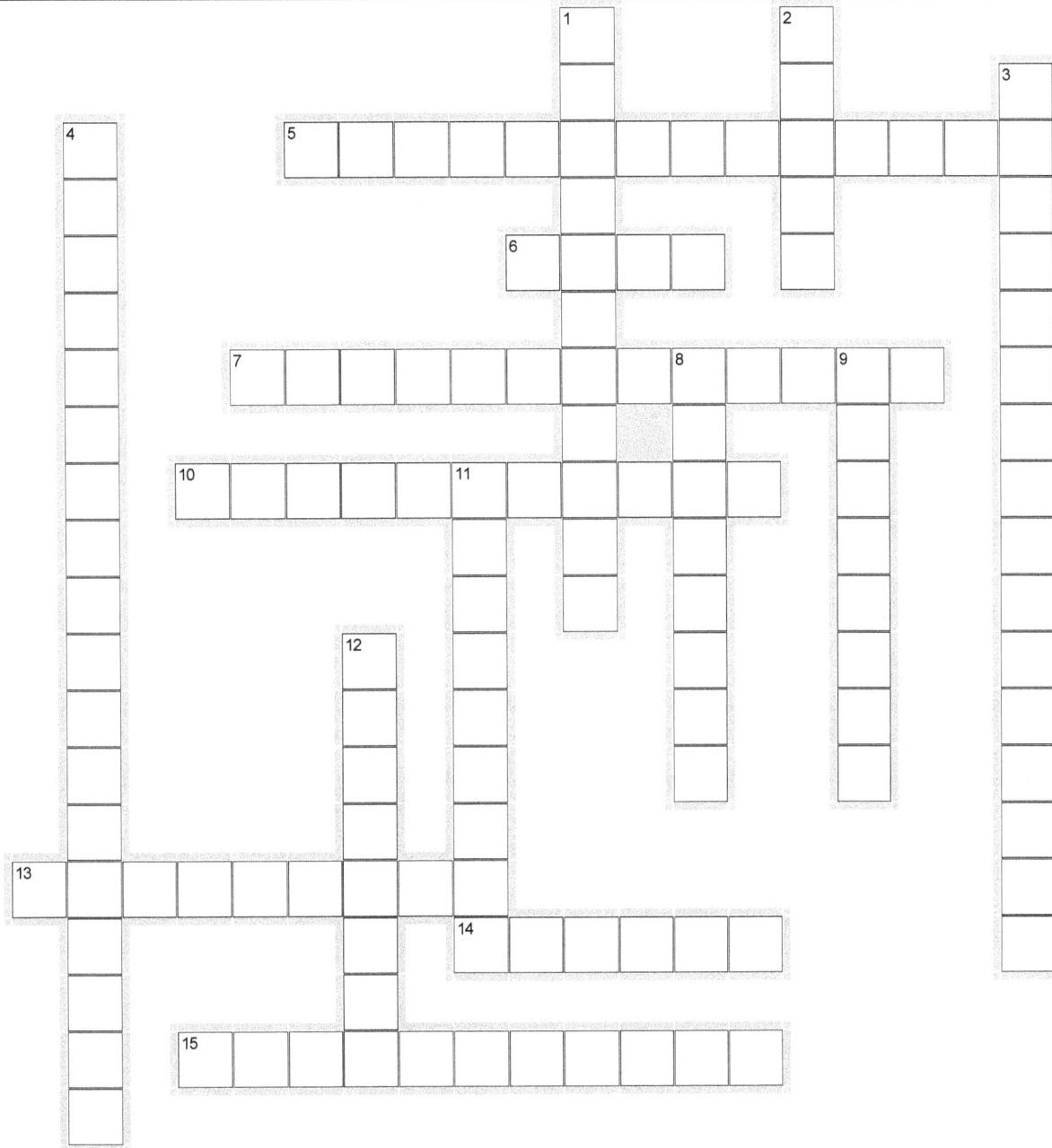

EclipseCrossword.com

Word List

Artifacts   Burial File   Citation   Evidence
Fact   Hidden Source   Historical Context   Home Source
Interment   Memorabilia   Obituary   Primary Source
Proof   Secondary Source   Source

Across

5.   A piece of evidence from the past that was created during the event.
6.   Something that actually exists; truth; reality.
7.   A source of information you might not automatically think of when you search for family records.
10.   Items collected and kept because of personal or historical significance.
13.   Location where a person is buried.
14.   People, documents, artifacts, and print or digital materials.
15.   Document or clue found in your home.

Down

1.   A file created on a military man or woman who dies while in service.
2.   Evidence or argument establishing or helping to establish a fact or truth of a statement.
3.   Sources created after an event by people who do not have firsthand knowledge of the event.
4.   Placing a person in the time period in which they lived.
8.   Notice of someone's death in the newspaper.
9.   Bibliographic origin of evidence.
11.   Memorabilia passed down through the generations.
12.   Something that pertains to an issue in question.

Lesson 13: Vital Records

Goal

Understand the importance of vital records in genealogical research. Locate and use vital records.

Vocabulary

Birth Certificate: An official document issued when a person is born.

Death Certificate: An official document issued when a person dies.

Marriage License: An official document issued to a couple so they may be married.

Obituary: A notice placed in the newspaper about the death of an individual. Obituaries may include names of other family members, location of burial, employment and service organization memberships, and wake and funeral information.

Vital Records: Governmental records on life events such as birth certificates, marriage licenses, and death certificates.

Reading Assignment

Research Tip 8: Local Records by Raymond S. Wright III, Ph.D., AG on Genealogy.com
http://www.genealogy.com/tip8.html

Lesson

Vital records are governmental records on life events such as birth certificates, marriage licenses, and death certificates. These records help us establish proof of relationships between people in our family.

Early vital records contained less information than vital records of today. Records changed over time and became standardized in the United States. You can view today's standard certificates here:

Birth Certificate

http://www.cdc.gov/nchs/data/dvs/birth11-03final-acc.pdf

Death Certificate

http://www.cdc.gov/nchs/data/dvs/death11-03final-acc.pdf

How do these compare to earlier certificates you have located?

Birth certificate: An official document issued when a person is born. Let's look at an example of two birth certificates and compare the information. The certificates both state they are for Frank Kokoska but the author will show why this is not the case. It is important to reinforce the concept with children that not everything you see and hear is correct.

These certificates belong to the author's ancestors. Frank Kokoska and Charles Kokoska were brothers. They were born to Joseph and Majdalena, nee Priban, Kokoska. Majdalena was the mother of eleven children.

Example 1: Frank Kokoska

Look up Frank's birth certificate on FamilySearch.org.

1. Visit http://familysearch.org and scroll down to click "United States" under location.
2. Click on "Illinois" on the left column and then click "Illinois, Cook County Birth Certificates, 1878-1922."
3. Search for "Frank Kokoska" and click the certificate for the Frank born in 1882.
4. View the details and then click "View image" on the left side of the screen.
5. You should be looking at this **source:** Chicago, Illinois, Birth Certificate, certificate no. 12756, Frank Kokoska, microfilm no. 7/0048/03.

Facts: Frank Kokoska, male, white, second child of this mother, date of birth 20 October 1882 at 412 W. 17th St in Chicago. Parents are Majdalena Kokoska, nee Skryvan. Father Joseph Kokoska, a laborer.

Analysis: Frank was the second child born to Majdalena and Joseph Kokoska. His birth date and place was confirmed through draft registrations and death records. Majdalena's maiden name which the certificate notes as Skryvan is incorrect. Her maiden name was Priban.

Discuss: What other details do you see on this birth certificate? List them here:

_____

_____

_____

_____

_____

Example 2: Charles Kokoska

Look up Charles' birth certificate on FamilySearch.org. His certificate however, is listed under Frank Kokoska born 1886.

1. Visit http://familysearch.org and scroll down to click "United States" under location.
2. Click on "Illinois" on the left column and then click "Illinois, Cook County Birth Certificates, 1878-1922."
3. Search for "Frank Kokoska" and click the certificate for the Frank born in 1886.
4. View the details and then click "View image" on the left side of the screen.
5. You should be looking at this **source:** Chicago, Illinois, Birth Certificate, certificate no. 97986, Frank Kokoska, microfilm no. 7/0048/03.

Facts: Frank Kokoska, male, white, fifth child of this mother, date of birth 27 January 1886 at 691 May St in Chicago. Parents are Majdalena Kokoska, nee Trivian. Father Joseph Kokoska, a laborer.

Analysis: This certificate actually belongs to Frank's brother Charles. The certificate says it is also for a Frank Kokoska, but the midwife, or whoever wrote the information down, wrote down the wrong name. The child is actually Charles. This is proven through additional records such as census, death certificates, and World War I Draft Registration Cards.

This child is also listed as the fifth child born to this family. Based on the author's research, the children born prior to Charles were Joseph, Frank, and Emilie. So, Charles would have been the fourth child.

Discussion: Explore these birth certificates in more detail. Do you notice anything else different about them? What would you do if you located these birth certificates without having any other records or information to prove the second certificate was not for Charles? Would you take it as fact or note it in your records with the source and review the certificates later when you found more information?

_____

_____

_____

_____

_____

Example 2: Marriage license

A **marriage license** is an official document issued to a couple so they may be married. Marriage licenses and certificates can sometimes tell you a lot about a family, depending on when and where they were created. Some certificates will have additional documents attached indicating the names of the bride and groom's parents, the bride and groom's dates and places of birth, names of witnesses, and their ages. This information can sometimes help prove or disprove a marriage license is for your family.

Example: Let's look at a Chicago marriage license from 1907.

Look up Jaroslav Darda's marriage licence on FamilySearch.org.

1. Visit http://familysearch.org and scroll down to click "United States" under location.
2. Click on "Illinois" on the left column and then click "Illinois, Cook County Marriages, 1871-1920."
3. Search for "Jaroslav Darda" and click the certificate for Jaroslav and Marie Kakuska.
4. View the details and then click "View image" on the left side of the screen.
5. You should be looking at this **source:** Chicago, Illinois, Marriage license, certificate no. 455213, Jaroslav Darda, microfilm no. 7/0039/02.

Facts: A marriage license was issued on 20 April 1907 for Jaroslav Darda, age 24, and Miss Marie Kakuska, age 19. The couple was married on 27 April 1907 by a minister of the Bohemian Congregation of Freethinkers.

Analysis: Marie's last name is misspelled. It was actually Kokoska. She is a sister to Frank and Charles. Additionally, verifying these people are the same people in the author's tree would require examining any of the following: birth certificates, census records, family Bible, interviews, and other sources. Knowing the faith or specific church in which they were married allows the author to possibly examine the church records for more details.

Discussion: Show your child your marriage license and, if possible, your parents' or grandparents' license if they have it. How are they the same? How are they different? What information do they contain that you can add to your family history notes? Finally, how do they compare to the license from 1907?
Always keep in mind that names are not spelled the same in every document that you will encounter. Watch for name variations and nicknames.

_____

_____

_____

_____

_____

Example 3: Death Certificate

Death certificate: An official document issued when a person dies.

Example: Death certificate of Helen Holik in 1912.

Look up Helen Holik's death certificate on FamilySearch.org.

1. Visit http://familysearch.org and scroll down to click "United States" under location.
2. Click on "Illinois" on the left column and then click "Illinois, Cook County Deaths, 1878-1922."
3. Search for "Helen Holik" and click the certificate.
4. View the details and then click "View image" on the left side of the screen.
5. You should be looking at this **source:** Chicago, Illinois, Death Certificate, certificate no. 21452, Helen Holik, Cook County Clerk's Office, Chicago.

Facts: Helen Holik was listed as a female, single, born in Chicago 19 November 1911. She was 8 years and 26 days old. She died on 15 Aug 1912 at 5:30 pm. Her father is listed as Jan Holik from Bohemia. Her mother is listed as Mary Rataj from Bohemia. The death occurred at 3154 So Ridgway Ave. She was buried at Boh Nat on 18 August 1912. Cause of death is listed as pneumonia.

Analysis: First, let's assume no birth certificate was located since vital records were not required in Illinois until 1916. Helen's birth and death fell in between census years so we cannot attempt to verify any information to a census record. We can take this information and add it to the family group sheets with each fact cited as to where the information was obtained.

If a birth certificate was located then we can compare the birth date, parents' names, and birth places to that of her death certificate. If she had been born and lived through a census year, provided a census record could be located, we could then compare this information against that record.

Discussion: What other facts are found on the death certificate that are not listed above? How can these facts help you identify other places to look for records?

_____

_____

_____

_____

_____

_____

Example: Death Certificate

Search for Thomas Fratto's death certificate on FamilySearch.org.

Source: "Illinois, Cook County Death Certificates," for Thomaso Fratto; death certificate no. 33905, Chicago, Illinois.

Facts: Thomaso Fratto was living at 2971 Wentworth Ave, Chicago. He was born 17 Dec 1876 in Taverna, Italy. He died 17 Dec 1935 in Chicago, IL. He was married to Theresa. He was a butcher. His father was Fortunato Fratto. His mother was Carmina LaFore/LaFare. Both were born in Taverna, Italy. He is buried at Mount Carmel Cemetery.

Analysis: This is another example of a death certificate. Many clues can be pulled from this record besides the above. Note the certificate informant was a hospital staff member. Do you think she knew Thomaso personally? Do you think she obtained his information from his hospital entrance record? What else can you find on this record that will expand what is known about this person?

Notes on Vital Records
Vital records were not always a requirement in the U.S. Each state began requiring records to be kept at different times.

Be aware that in addition to the variety of dates in which each state enacted a requirement for vital records registration, state and county boundaries have also changed over time. Knowing where your ancestors lived can help you locate where records can be found. By

using maps such as the Newberry Library's Atlas of History County Boundaries Map you can explore boundary shifts from the beginning of the state formation to the present day. As county boundaries changed, the location of records changed.
http://publications.newberry.org/ahcbp/

Another consideration when locating vital records is the possibility of destruction by fire, flood, or war. Many courthouses have had fires that wiped out all records, many of which may not be found anywhere else. When you come across a county like this, look for other record sources that may help you verify the information that you already have or that could help you locate new information.

Make it Personal

Choose one ancestral line and use the Newberry Library's Atlas of Historical County Boundaries Map found here, http://publications.newberry.org/ahcbp/ to explore boundary shifts from the beginning of the state formation to the present day for that line of ancestors. Search history books and websites to find out, if possible, why the boundaries changed for state or county. Was this due to the expansion of the state? Was this due to the division of a state such as when Virginia was broken into Virginia and West Virginia?

Attempt to determine if any of your ancestors' records were destroyed by fire, flood, or war. Another possibility is the records were not being recorded and stored. Use history resources and *Red Book: American State, County, and Town Sources* to explore the events surrounding the destruction or creation of the original documents.

Assignment

Part I: Locate vital records in your home. Examine the facts and add the information with source citations to your family group sheets.

Part II: Visit FamilySearch.org's website to see if there are vital records for your ancestors online. http://familysearch.org Remember that not all records have been digitized and made available online. Download and save any vital records you locate. Make sure you record the source for each record in your notebook or on a printout of the document.

Optional: Search the newspapers where your ancestors lived for obituaries. Check with your local library to see if they have any of these papers available online or microfilm.

Lesson 14: Census Records

Goal

Understand the value of census records for research. Learn where to find census records and how to search them for ancestors. *Note: The 1890 Census was mostly lost due to fire.

Vocabulary

Census: An official count of a population which records specific details about individuals and families.

Enumeration: A numbered list of data.

Enumeration District: A geographic region defined as a tract, area, or district, in which a census is taken.

Reading Assignment

Every Ten Years: Key to the United States Census, 1790-1930 by Genealogy.com
http://www.genealogy.com/13_every.html

Secrets of the Census by Donna Pzrecha on Genealogy.com
http://www.genealogy.com/13_secrt.html

Lesson

The U.S. Census is an incredible tool used by genealogists to help prove relationships, migration patterns, and other facts recorded in their family histories. Historians and other researchers use the **census** as a way to statistically document immigration, migration, local and state history, ethnicity, economics, and other issues.

What is the census? It is a count of all the people living in the United States, town by town. The government uses this information to decide where to build more schools, more roads, and where to provide more money and resources.

Historical Background

The U.S. Census was first taken in 1790 after an Article was added to the U.S. Constitution requiring a count of the nation's individuals every ten years. The first census had only six questions. Enumerators were required to record only the name of the family head. It would not be until 1850 when all individuals in a family would be recorded on a U.S. Census. The first census also required the number of free white males broken into two categories - sixteen years and older, and free white males under sixteen. This helped the government identify potential military-aged men. The number of free white females, other persons, and slaves was recorded without age distinction. In some cases the town or district of residence was also recorded.

Until 1850, the census listed the head of the family and a count of others in the household. In 1850 and future censuses, the names of all individuals were added. By 1880, the street name was added with a house number. These addresses are important to keep track of in your notes. They can help you locate people in other records or help prove the person you found is the one you are looking for.

Locating Census Records

Where can you find the census? Online subscription sites like Ancestry.com, Fold3.com, and Archives.com hold census records. There are also free sites like FamilySearch.org and Heritage Quest (usually available through your local library) that offer census records. Ancestry.com can also be found for free use through most local libraries.

Repositories like the National Archives and local research libraries also carry the census on microfilm. Sometimes local genealogy societies will transcribe the records and publish them in books or journals.

Census Searching Strategies

Each census index located online was transcribed by different individuals. No two indexes are exactly alike. You might have difficulty locating an ancestor through one index only to find them in another. In addition, one indexer may read a name one way and another indexer may see it completely different if it was not written neatly on the census sheet.

Try a variety of spellings when looking for ancestors. If you are not exactly sure how a surname was spelled, or perhaps it was spelled differently over time, try a wildcard search. A wildcard search means to use an * after part of the word you are searching. For example, I have a surname Kokoska. In an Ancestry.com search I might have no luck finding that surname in a particular census for the Chicago area. I could type 'Koko*' in the surname box, add a first name and other information and see what the search results provide.

Also try a variety of search criteria. Sometimes the search engine will not be able to find your head of household. Try searching for the wife or a child. Add as much information as possible to your search. This means to add the names of all siblings, the location where the family was living, birth year or full birth date, and immigration date if that is an option.

Check the search results. If the results do not yield the information you seek, try removing some of the search criteria. Sometimes less is more. Other times more is what you need.

There are times when our ancestors do not appear on a census when we believe they should. There could be many reasons for this.

- They were serving in the military and were not in the country when the census was taken.
- They lived somewhere other than where we thought they should be living.
- The name was spelled so incorrectly that indexes do not find them in a search.
- The family was migrating from one location to another.

Assignment

Part I: Examine your pedigree chart(s) and identify each census year through 1940 in which your ancestors may be found. Write the results as follows listing the number of the person in your main line, his or her name and the years they lived (birth – death). Then list each census in which they may be found and where you think you may find them based on addresses and other information you have collected.

> No. 4 Joseph John Holik (1906-1964)
> 1910 – Cook Co., IL
> 1920 – Cook Co., IL
> 1930 – Cook Co., IL

Part II: Search online census databases for some of these records. Many subscription sites offer a free trial period. Consider signing up for one or more of these so you can search from home. Another option is to visit your local library and use the subscription sites there.

Places to locate online census information:

Ancestry.com   http://ancestry.com
FamilySearch   http://familysearch.org
Fold3.com   http://fold3.com

Your local library may offer Heritage Quest access from home.

Additional Resources

U.S. Census Bureau Kid's Census Corner
http://factfinder.census.gov/home/en/kids/kids.html

Lesson 15: Start a Diary

Goal

Begin recording your thoughts, current local and world events, and information about your life.

Items Needed

Journal: A diary, notebook, or other book in which to record your thoughts.

Lesson

We talked about Hidden Sources in a prior lesson. One of those sources was a diary. Do you have a diary? If not, why? Diaries can be a rich source of family history information.

Diaries can help you learn about:
- The daily life of an ancestor
- The cost of food and supplies
- Information about relationships, both familial and friends
- Local and world history facts.

Assignment

Help your child start a diary. Put their name inside the cover and have them date each entry they write. As you work through your genealogy projects they should write their thoughts in the diary. Encourage the child to draw or cut out pictures to glue in the diary to go along with their writing.

Your child does not have to write in the diary every day. This is just a writing exercise to help them continue creative writing and to learn to record details of their lives.

Need some ideas about what to write?
- Things you did today
- Your best friends
- Things you are good at
- Your goals
- Where you want to go on vacation
- What your house looks like
- Talk about your parents and siblings
- Special memories of time spent with grandparents
- Your favorite subjects in school

- Books you love
- Your dreams.

If your child is active in Boy Scouts, Girl Scouts, 4-H, American Heritage, or other scouting groups, find out if you can use some of the lessons in this book toward earning a badge. Boy Scouts must keep a journal for six weeks as part of their requirements. This assignment will help them earn that portion of their badge.

Review: Lessons 13 to 15

Crossword Vocabulary Review

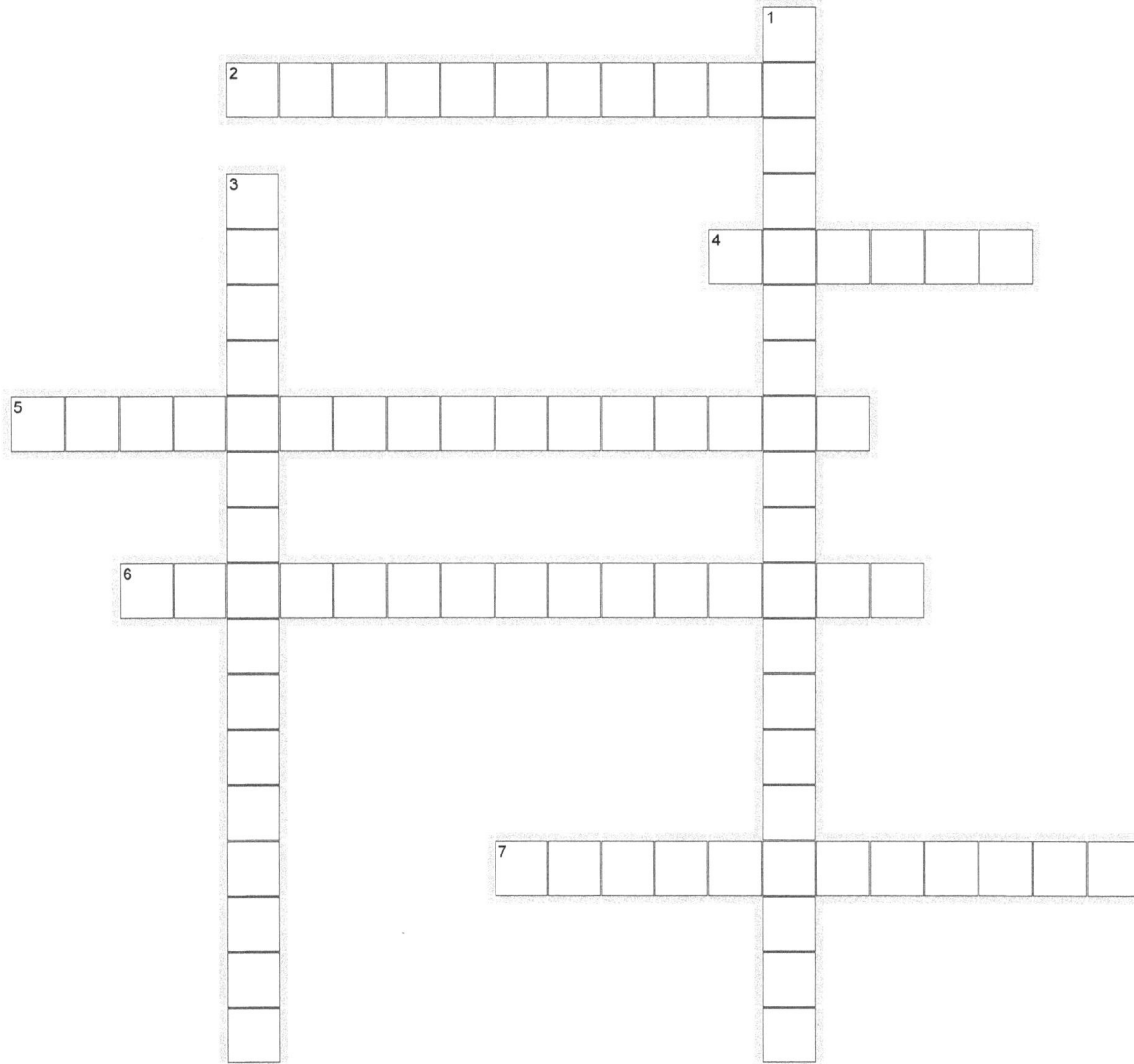

© 2018 Jennifer Holik World War II Research & Writing Center

EclipseCrossword.com

Word List

Birth Certificate   Census   Death Certificate   Enumeration
Enumeration District   Marriage License   Vital Records

Across

2.   A numbered list of data.
4.   An official count of a population which records specific details about individuals and families.
5.   An official document issued when a person dies.
6.   An official document issued to a couple so they may be married.
7.   Governmental records on life events such as birth certificates, marriage licenses, and death
       certificates.

Down

1.   A geographic region defined as a tract, area, or district, in which a census is taken.
3.   An official document issued when a person is born.

Final Project Lessons 1-15

Option 1:

Create a family story on a poster board.

Items needed

Poster board	Photographs	Glue or tape
Pencils	Markers	All charts and records found to date

Choose one family on your pedigree chart, and create a story about them on the poster board. For example, this could be the family of your paternal great grandparents.

Your project should include:

- A title
- Photographs or drawings of the family you chose
- Photographs of artifacts and/or photocopies of documents you discovered
- Vital information such as birth, marriage and death dates and places (if known)
- Facts about the family you discovered
- Cite the sources for the facts you list on the back of the poster board
- Your signature and the date of completion the back of the poster board
- A three to four-page story about your board and the ancestors featured.

Let the child be as creative as they want. They may choose to make a family tree with the family on it somewhere on the board and then write the facts about their lives. Copies of documents may be placed elsewhere to help prove the facts they wrote. Or, you may choose to divide the board into four sections and add photographs in one, facts in another, a story in a third, and copies of documents in the final section.

Option 2:

Create a PowerPoint presentation at least 15 slides long that discuss one family in your pedigree chart. For example, this could be the family of your paternal great grandparents.

Your story should include:

- A title
- Photographs or drawings of the family you chose
- Vital information such as birth, marriage and death dates and places (if known)
- Facts about the family you discovered
- Photographs of artifacts and/or photocopies of documents you discovered
- A story about the family.

Lesson 16: Health and the Mysteries of Death

Goal

Examine the health and cause of death of each ancestor in your direct line. Understand why a health history family tree is important.

Vocabulary

Collateral Lines: A line of descent connecting persons who share a common ancestor. These individuals are related through an aunt, uncle, or cousin.

Death Certificate: An official document issued upon a person's death. Certificates usually include the individual's name, date and place of birth, date and place of death, names of parents, cause of death, and location of burial.

Epidemic: A widespread occurrence of an infectious disease. This usually occurs in a community during a specific time period.

Reading Assignment

Mayo Clinic *Medical History: Compiling your medical family tree*
http://www.mayoclinic.com/health/medical-history/HQ01707

The U.S. Department of Health & Human Services *Surgeon General's Family Health History* http://www.hhs.gov/familyhistory/

Lesson

MYSTERY: What caused their death?

Many different things caused the death of our ancestors. Death certificates, obituaries, and family stories are all ways to discover the cause of death. Have you ever stopped to consider if the things your family members died of were hereditary? Are certain conditions passed down through the generations?

Diseases like cancer, diabetes, thyroid disease, and heart disease as well as conditions like depression, autism, and ADHD can run in families. Rarer diseases like sickle cell anemia and hemophilia may also run in families. Understanding and recording the cause of death for not only your direct line but also your collateral lines will help you have a clearer picture of diseases that may run in your family.

When you visit the doctor today, a medical history is taken not only for you but also your family. Ask your parents if they have completed a medical history at their doctor's office recently. Ask them how often they have to update this information. Is it only once a year or each visit?

Most doctors have questions that list a long list of diseases, such as the ones listed above, which you should mark if they have run in your family. This not only includes your direct line but also collaterals as well. This medical history helps the doctors treat you for current ailments and also help you try to prevent, or catch early, future ailments or issues.

For example, if heart disease runs in your family, your doctor may suggest exercise, vitamins, cholesterol checks, and healthy eating. If thyroid disease runs in your family then yearly blood draws to check thyroid levels may be suggested.

Assignment

Part I: Retrieve the death certificates you have located to date. If you do not have many certificates yet, ask your parents and grandparents about relatives who have died and find out the cause of death. Create a list that contains:

- Name of deceased
- Date of birth
- Date of death
- Cause of death
- Contributory factors or causes.

Do you see any trends? Did one cause of death seem to be prevalent? Did that cause run down a specific line in the family?

Part II: Read Genealogy Quest's "American Epidemics" page and see if the death records you hold fall into any epidemic time period.
http://www.genealogy-quest.com/glossaries/epidemics.html

Part III: Create a family health history. Visit My Family Health History at
https://familyhistory.hhs.gov/fhh-web/home.action and fill in the blanks to create your family health history.

Save this history and print a copy for your binder.

Additional Resources

Daus, Carol. *Past Imperfect*. Santa Monica: Santa Monica Press, 1999.

Gormley, Myra Vanderpool. *Family Diseases Are You at Risk?* Baltimore: Genealogical Publishing Company, 1989.

Cause of Death Word Search

```
S C M Y T I G J C M D Y Y A K A R A D U L L P S E
A I O J E A H Q H X X X G N K I W M J O G U E H D
R Y S L W Y L M O E A R G A D O P E C S Y P Y E E
L G V O I F F O L M U Q E Z L N J K B D T T X A M
G S A K R C X P E F D J J F O F J W A I G U G T A
N U I P Y E O O R B G C X P O A H C C B J O P S Q
N Y F M S P L W A A U S Q O W M X I S T B Z C T Q
O L R A A H A C R G V R M R K B M Z A Z W D U R S
I F V E T N I B S N Z B U L A I Q G V U V L G O I
T V C V T T T N H O Z N V C A W H N H Q G B S K S
P V R H W N Y X G U I X D S A I R E H T P I D E O
M Y I M B K E L U L B R I J A U N D I C E A Z D R
U H P B U T H S I I E T E T Y P H U S K G V K B H
S F T A L Q W O Y V I S M T V T V C Z U M D P J P
N E X E H Q E Y N D E L Q C R S G Y E B M I Y Z E
O J F E T P N R R C E R X H E A E J R T R V T H N
C V S V O V P A A B P Z D A X U Q C G Z R Q O R R
V G A Q C H C L T R X A E K G T D K U U S Q W V Q
X B G M K O V M L W Z W C S F B Z T C F Y E B W L
I Z B Y Y W I N T E R F E V E R Y S U U G U D B S
B W R M T L H Z L S T E I A E X S M Y Q E X E L M
D C E H A Z H N R D U O B N D J N L H L W D F Z M
R L W H E O Z W V S G W T K Z O I D Y R W L R X H
B D O M G Q H U Y Z G F H N X K U F K M H E C D M
G C X J M Z L A N U M X J I A D Q L C E R Y E C K
```

AGUE
APOPLEXY
ARTERIOSCLEROSIS
CHOLERA
COLIC
CONSUMPTION
DIPTHERIA
DYSENTERY
EDEMA
FATTY LIVER
HEAT STROKE
JAUNDICE
LOCK JAW
MYOCARDITIS

NEPHROSIS
PODAGRA
QUINSY
RUBEOLA
SCURVY
SEPTICIMIA
SHINGLES
TYPHUS
WINTER FEVER

Definitions:

AGUE:

APOPLEXY:

ARTERIOSCLEROSIS:

CHOLERA:

COLIC:

CONSUMPTION:

DIPTHERIA:

DYSENTERY:

EDEMA:

FATTY LIVER:

HEAT STROKE:

JAUNDICE:

LOCK JAW:

MYOCARDITIS:

NEPHROSIS:

PODAGRA:

QUINSY:

RUBEOLA:

SCURVY:

SEPTICIMIA:

SHINGLES:

TYPHUS:

WINTER FEVER:

Lesson 17: Occupations

Goal

Examine the jobs your ancestors held.

Vocabulary

Occupation: A job.

Reading Assignment

Cyndi's List – Occupations Section is full of resources on the names of occupations past and present. http://www.cyndislist.com/occupations/general/

Lesson

Find the census records you viewed and the records you located in your home sources and hidden sources assignments. Discuss how the jobs of your ancestors compare to the jobs your parents and grandparents do today. The Occupation List on Rootsweb in your reading assignment provides a great list of occupation titles and what they mean. For instance, did you know an accountant used to be called an accomptant? How about a bar tender as an ale draper? A parish man or what we might call a minister or priest was referred to as an amen man.

Make it Personal

After completing the assignment, write a one-page report on interesting jobs your ancestors held. Are they jobs you would consider doing? What is the reason they worked in certain fields? Did they migrate across the U.S. to seek new employment? Why? During the Great Depression many people left their homes and moved to find jobs. See if there are major historical events that caused your family to move and change jobs.

Assignment

Part I: Examine the census transcriptions you made. Choose one direct line to evaluate. Make a list of the individuals in that line and their occupations. Note the year of the census where the information appeared. Do any jobs appear repeatedly in that family line?

Part II: Complete the word search on the next page. Then define the words on the page that follows.

Occupation Word Search

```
H N A M G A B R Q A V R R C N J R T R R
R T B X W H E A P D O E A F A O E I E S
E L I J D F O P R T W R X R M Y K N V M
J R M M F R R O A N W E V H N R K E I
R B O U S E A G F I B P G A C E A E B T
R E L T N D I G F E P A A C T R P R B H
N B K T A V E E O I R N L C A M A W E R
X A I R A R X R D O L A D O W V N V B L
U C M N A A E S P A N M E M F A R M E R
E O C L E B H M G Z V O R P P F K E D B
A A B O I R V G U Y A W M T L U Z Y T Q
W E K H I O E P I N A S A A O M D T D R
R K R E C R E M S B E D N N W A H N O T
M E V O N A C L U V P A O T M B Y T O R
E E L F N H C O L L I E R F A U S P G E
U C L A T A H U U R Q H Q C N A M L L T
C H J Q B Y U J K Z T A N O P A L Q S N
E M H S H Z I T H E R I S T N W G X T A
Q H T I M S N W O R B N A M S D A O L C
S A W Y E R O F L T W Q J T T P W E X A
```

ACCOMPTANT	DRAGOON	PASTOR
AERONAUT	ENUMERATOR	PLOWMAN
ALDERMAN	FARMER	REDSMITH
APPRENTICE	FOWER	SAWYER
BAGMAN	HEADSWOMAN	SHRIEVE
BALER	HOOFER	SMITH
BARKER	JOYNER	TINKER
BEVER	LAGGER	TOPMAN
BLUFFER	LOADSMAN	VULCAN
BROWNSMITH	MAWER	WATCHMAN
CANTER	MERCER	ZITHERIST
CARNIFEX	NAVIGATOR	
COLLIER	OILMAN	
DIPPER	PARKER	

Definitions:

ACCOMPTANT:	HOOFER:
AERONAUT:	JOYNER:
ALDERMAN:	LAGGER:
APPRENTICE:	LOADSMAN:
BAGMAN:	MAWER:
BALER:	MERCER:
BARKER:	NAVIGATOR:
BEVER:	OILMAN:
BLUFFER:	PARKER:
BROWNSMITH:	PASTOR:
CANTER:	PLOWMAN:
CARNIFEX:	REDSMITH:
COLLIER:	SAWYER:
DIPPER:	SHRIEVE:
DRAGOON:	SMITH:
ENUMERATOR:	TINKER:
FARMER:	TOPMAN:
FOWER:	VULCAN:
HEADSWOMAN:	WATCHMAN:
	ZITHERIST:

Lesson 18: Probate Records

Goal

Learn basic details about probate records and how these records are useful.

Vocabulary

Intestate: When someone dies without a will.

Probate: Legal process of settling an estate.

Proof of Heirship: Testimony documenting the relationships of heirs listed in a probate file to the deceased.

Testate: When someone dies with a will.

Testator: One who creates a will.

Will: Document in which a Testator disburses his estate, both real and personal property.

Reading Assignment

Wills and Testaments by Donna Pzrecha on Genealogy.com
http://www.genealogy.com/46_donna.html

Lesson

Records are continually being created for individuals from the time they are born until the time they die. One set of records that may be created are **probate** records. Included in probate records are **wills** and **Proof of Heirship** testimony. When a person dies without a will, that estate is classified as **intestate**. When a person dies with a will, that estate is classified as **testate.**

An Example of the Process

When a person ages they might create a will. Someone who creates a will is called a **testator.** A will explains what the person wants to give to his or her spouse, children, relatives, and possibly associations and organizations to which he belongs.

Example of a Will

I, John Smith, being of sound mind and body hereby declare this to be my last Will and Testament, thereby revoking any former Wills.

First, To my wife Betsy Smith, I bequeath all of my personal and real property. In the event she predecease me, all of my person and real property will be divided between my three children, Albert Smith, Sarah Smith and Kevin Smith, share and share alike.

Second, I request that the amount of $500 be given as a donation to the St. Mary Church in Riverside, Illinois.

Third, I request that the amount of $500 be given as a donation to the American Cancer Society in my name.

Fourth, I appoint as my executrix, my wife Betsy Smith. In the event she predecease me, then I appoint my son Albert Smith as executor.

That is a very brief example of a will. They can be very complex listing multiple items to be distributed. But, wills contain a lot of clues about the family of the deceased. You may find people named and their relationship to the deceased. From the example above, you know that at the time John wrote his will he was married to Betsy Smith. You also know he lists his children as Albert, Sarah, and Kevin. What the will does not tell you is if they are his natural born children or if they are adopted. The will provides an idea, depending on how detailed it is, of how wealthy the individual may have been.

During the probate process, the will is entered into the Probate Court and must undergo a process to be approved. Then the heirs must be verified through a process called Proof of Heirship.

The Proof of Heirship is testimony given by one or more individuals specifically naming the heirs of the deceased, their age, name of spouse if married, and information about the deceased and his spouse.

Proof of Heirship testimony can help researchers identify new family members, connect a married name to a woman, and verify known family members. The ages provided also help narrow down a year of birth if one was previously unknown. The addresses will help you track these families in census records and other documents. Proof of Heirship is an invaluable piece of the researcher's puzzle.

Probate records entail more than the documents described above and all the pieces together, really paint the picture of part of the life of an individual.

Assignment

Part I: Put on your detective hat and look for clues! Read the example Proof of Heirship below. What clues can you find for this family? Can you find:
- The name of the deceased
- The date of his death
- The name of the woman giving testimony
- The address of the woman giving testimony
- The name of his wife
- Names and number of children born to Daniel

COURT: Please give your name and relationship to the deceased.

WOMAN: My name is Susan Jones and Daniel Howard was my father.

COURT: What is your address?

WOMAN: 464 E. State St., Pontiac, WI

COURT: When did Daniel Howard die?

WOMAN: On April 24, 1902.

COURT: Was he married?

WOMAN: No, he was widowed.

COURT: His wife predeceased him? What was her name and when did she die?

WOMAN: Her name was Elizabeth Howard. She died May 28, 1899.

COURT: How many children were born to Elizabeth and Daniel Howard?

WOMAN: Six.

COURT: Name them.

WOMAN: Frank, Robert, Catherine, two babies who died, and myself.

COURT: Were there any others born to this union?

WOMAN: No.

Part II: Read the will again and locate the following:
- Name of the testator
- Name of his wife
- Names of his children
- Number of children
- Amount of money he was giving to St. Mary's Church.

I, John Smith, being of sound mind and body hereby declare this to be my last Will and Testament, thereby revoking any former Wills.

First, To my wife Betsy Smith, I bequeath all of my personal and real property. In the event she predecease me, all of my person and real property will be divided between my three children, Albert Smith, Sarah Smith and Kevin Smith, share and share alike.

Second, I request that the amount of $500 be given as a donation to St. Mary's Church in Riverside, Illinois.

Third, I appoint as my executrix, my wife Betsy Smith. In the event she predecease me, then I appoint my son Albert Smith as executor.

Lesson 19: Land Records and Maps

Goal

Learn how land records and maps can help you bring your family to life and lead you down new research paths.

Vocabulary

Affidavit: An oath made before any person who is authorized to record an oath.

Deed: A written legal document that authorizes the transfer of property.

Grantee: Purchaser of property.

Grantor: Seller of property.

Map: Representation of an area of land or sea showing physical features such as cities, roads, mountains, etc.

Migration: The movement of individuals or families from one locale to another.

Reading Assignment

Analyzing Maps
http://www.loc.gov/teachers/usingprimarysources/resources/Analyzing_Maps.pdf

Atlas of Historical County Boundaries   http://publications.newberry.org/ahcbp/

Croom, Emily Anne. *The Genealogist's Companion and Sourcebook.* Cincinnati: Betterway Books, 2003.
    Read Deed Records, pgs. 101-110.

Lesson

Land records can tell us a lot about a family and the life they led. Land records may provide proof of family relationships between parent and child or extended family members. They provide a legal description of the property. These descriptions enable researchers to draw them out on a **map** or sheet of paper. Those drawings can be incorporated into published family histories or genealogy databases.

Deeds are an important part of genealogical research because they can provide clues to new family members or relationships between people. There are many parts of a deed that aid the research we conduct. Let's examine each of these.

- **Names of the Parties:** The names of the **grantors** (sellers) and **grantees** (buyers) are listed at the top of a deed. In many cases where a husband and wife are selling or buying a piece of property, that relationship will be noted.

- **Legal Description of Land:** This is a very important piece of a deed. It specifically outlines the exact location of the piece of property being transferred. This legal description can help you locate that property on a map and possibly obtain additional information from the Recorder of Deeds Office where deeds and other records are held.

- **Signatures or Marks:** Did your ancestor know how to sign his name or did he use a mark [X] as his signature? Deeds will show you the answer to this question. Signatures are a good thing to collect so you can compare them against other documents, especially if you are trying to determine if that John Smith is your John Smith.

- **Witnesses:** Witnesses were often family, friends, or neighbors. While the deed will not specify the relationship, knowing who these collateral people were can help you in future research. These clues may help you trace the **migration** of a family or locate them on a census if you are having difficulty locating your family.

- **Recording:** When and where was the deed recorded? Who notarized it and recorded it? As with witnesses, the names of the notary or Recorder or County Clerk may be family, friends, or neighbors. This is especially true in times when counties and towns were very young and had a low population.

Locating as many deeds as possible for your family can help paint a clearer picture of the living patterns of your family. Organizing by date will also help you trace the migration or expansion or addition of property. Keep in mind that just because someone owned a piece of land did not always mean they actually lived on it. Some farmers owned several tracts of land in a county and may have used that for livestock or crops.

As we move to maps, we can use many of the legal descriptions from the deeds to locate the property where our ancestors lived or owned land. Maps are useful because they give us a visual idea of where our ancestors lived, where they moved, and provide possible migration trails and patterns.

An important concept to remember when it comes to maps is that since the creation of the United States, county and state boundaries have changed many times. Use the Atlas of Historical County Boundaries http://publications.newberry.org/ahcbp/ to examine your state and county to see how it has changed since 1790 (the earliest date available) or the creation of your state and county.

Maps can also be used to trace migration from one place to another. You may not always know the exact route taken by an ancestor who migrated from Virginia to Kentucky to Missouri. You can examine a map and plot out where your ancestors lived in each state and connect the dots to have a visual idea of where they lived and how they might have migrated.

Make it Personal

Write down where you live or the places you have lived during your lifetime. Now list all the places your parents and grandparents lived. Create a list of questions that help form a plan to find out why each individual lived where they did. Consider why they may have moved, if they moved, as well as the employment they held while living in those locations. Add major world or local events to this list that may have created a reason for people to move from place to place.

Ask your parents and extended family the questions. How many answers can you get?

Discussion

Was your county part of other counties before it was officially named the county in which you live? What other counties did it belong to prior to the official formation?

Use the Atlas of Historical County Boundaries to learn the answers to these questions. http://publications.newberry.org/ahcbp/

Assignment

Part I: Write a report about the questions and answers you received in the Make It Personal section of this lesson. Include in your report the names of the people interviewed, the places they lived, and especially any historical events that caused the moves or gave them a reason to remain where they were.

Part II: Examine the following deed. Extract the following information and write a paragraph outlining the information.

- Grantor
- Grantee
- Witnesses
- Recorder's name
- Notary's name
- Consideration (amount of sale)
- Legal description
- Date of recording

162

sealed and delivered the said instrument as their free and voluntary act, for the uses and purposes therein set forth, including the release and waiver of the right of homestead.

Given under my hand and Notarial Seal, this 5th day of April. A.D. 1922.

L. J. Arnstein

Notary Public.

Leopold J. Arnstein
Notary Public
Cook County, Ill.
17---No. 7455742 Filed for Record Apr. 7 A.D. 1922 at 3:10 P.M.

JOSEPH P. HAAS, RECORDER.

The grantor, Jan Zajicek, widower, survivor of Dorota Zajicek, deceased, of the City of Chicago in the County of Cook and State of Illinois For And In Consideration of Tow Thousand ($2000.00) Dollars in hand paid, Conveys and Warrants to Joseph Kubat and Mary Kubat, his wife, of the City of Chicago County of Cook and State of Illinois as Joint Tenants, but not as tenants in common, the following described Real Estate, to wit:

The West Half (W.½) of Lot Twenty (20) in Block Four (4) in Johnson's subdivision of the North West Quarter (N.W.½) of the South West Quarter (S.W.½) of Section Nineteen (19) Township Thirty Nine (39) North, Range Fourteen (14) East of the Third Principal Meridian, together with all buildings and improvements thereon,

situated in the County of Cook in the State of Illinois, hereby releasing and waiving all rights under and by virtue of the Homestead Exemption Laws of the State of Illinois.

Subject to all taxes and special assessments due and payable after the year 1921.

Dated, this Thirty First day of January A.D. 1922.

Jan. Zajicek	(Seal)
	(Seal)
Jan Zajicek	(Seal)
	(Seal)

State of Illinois,)
) SS.
County of Cook,   )

I, Joseph A. Brabec, a Notary Public in and for, and residing in said County in the State aforesaid, Do Hereby Certify, that Jan Zajicek, widower, and survivor of Dorota Zajicek, deceased, personally known to me to be the same person whose name is subscribed to the foregoing instrument, appeared before me this day in person and acknowledged that he signed, sealed and delivered the said instrument as his free and voluntary act for the uses and purposes therein set forth, including the release and waiver of the right of homestead.

Given under my hand and Notarial Seal, this Sixth day of April A.D. 1922.

Joseph A. Brabec
Notary Public

Joseph A. Brabec
Notary Public
Cook County, Ill.
U. S. Rev. Stamp to the Amt. of $2.00 on this Inst.
5---No. 7455744 Filed for Record Apr. 7 A.D. 1922 at 3:11 P.M.

JOSEPH P. HAAS, RECORDER.

This Indenture Witnesseth, that the Grantor, Nellie Albrecht, a widow of the City

Source: Illinois, Cook County, Deed Book 17583:162, John Zajicek to Joseph Kubat and Mary Kubat; Office of the Recorder, Chicago.

Project - HistoryGeo

There is a relatively new website called HistoryGeo. The company released this information in early 2012. It is reprinted here with permission.

HistoryGeo.com opens its doors with the immediate inclusion of all the maps in both the *Family Maps* and *Texas Land Survey Maps* series of books. These represent nearly 40,000 maps among twenty-three states, all of which display original land-ownership in the context of modern roads, waterways, and other features.

In addition to Arphax's proprietary map library, over 2,000 historical land-ownership maps from Massachusetts, New York, Pennsylvania, Illinois, Indiana, Michigan, Ohio, Nebraska, and Kansas, have also been added. Plans are to increase the breadth of the HistoryGeo.com library to include all of the U.S. and eventually, the world.

With the HistoryGeo Viewer, users can:
- take Snapshots of locations in maps (similar to "favorites" or bookmarks)
- add Custom Markers to Maps, where you can attach:
    - your uploaded images,
    - links to HistoryGeo Snapshots, or
    - URLs to external web-content (link to web-pages of your choice)
- chart and animate migrations,
- designate their Markers as private, public, or to be shared only with friends
- search both within and outside HistoryGeo.com (GNIS searches included, for instance)

Subscriptions choices include a $44 quarterly account, a $66 semi-annual account, or a heavily-discounted choice of $99 per year (a 43% discount). People interested in this new service are recommended to do the following: 1) Register at www.historygeo.com and take a test drive with instant access to a number of free maps, and 2) take a look at the growing collection of instructional videos found at www.historygeo.com/videos. Once convinced that this is a service for you, simply click "Subscribe", and choose one of the three low-cost subscription options.

Investigate HistoryGeo as part of this lesson. Even if you do not have family who owned land and only lived in the city since immigration, it is still a great resource to explore.

Additional Resources

Hone, Wade E. *Land & Property Research in the United States.* Provo: Ancestry Publishing, 1997.

Kashuba, Melinda. *Walking with Your Ancestors A Genealogist's Guide to Using Maps and Geography.* Cincinnati: Family Tree Books, 2005.

Lesson 20: Military Records

Goal

Learn about military resources available to researchers and what those records contain.

Vocabulary

Burial File: A file compiled during World War I which documented the deaths and burials of U.S. soldiers who died while in service to their country. These documents sometimes contain letters from the family; disinterment records; service records; detailed cause of death; and health or state of the body information.

Draft Registration Cards: Military registration card documenting the vital information of an individual. Not all who registered for the draft fought and others who registered voluntarily enlisted to serve.

Enlistment Records: A record created on a military service man or woman at the time they joined the military.

Discharge Records: A record created on a military service man or woman at the time they left military service.

Individual Deceased Personnel File (IDPF): A file compiled during World War II and beyond which documented the deaths and burials of U.S. soldiers who died while in service to their country. These documents sometimes contain letters from the family; disinterment records; service records; detailed cause of death; and health or state of the body information. (See Burial File)

Military Records: A set of records compiled by the U.S. government regarding an individual's enlistment, service, and discharge from the armed forces.

Pension File: File containing documents pertaining to a set fee paid to a U.S. armed forces veteran for past service to the government. These records sometimes contain service information; birth, marriage and death records; family information; and health information.

State Bonus Applications: Application files for payments of a bonus to the soldier or his beneficiary after World War I and World War II. These records are typically held in State Archives.

Reading Assignment

Read the Memoirs and Diary of Private Jefferson Moses, Company G, 93rd Illinois Volunteers
http://www.ioweb.com/civilwar/

Lesson

Wars have been fought since the beginning of time. Records however have not been kept since the beginning of time. Where military records exist, you may find a goldmine of information. Military records can tell us a great deal about our ancestors and their families. But how do you know if you have a military ancestor? Here are a few ways to determine the possibility.

- Age at the time of the war, usually between the ages of 17 – 40 depending on the war. Sometimes younger.
- Examine county histories to see if your ancestor is mentioned.
- Look for siblings of your ancestors. Sometimes the ancestor in our direct line did not fight but a sibling did.
- Search the local newspaper for information on those who enlisted, died, or were discharged and sent home.

Types of Records Available

- Enlistment papers
  These records may contain vital information on an individual.

- Service records
  Service records outline the locations where a service man or woman served, honors and medals they received, and any disciplinary action taken against them.

- Discharge papers
  These records may provide vital information about the individual, dates of service, honorable or dishonorable discharge information, next of kin, and previous employment information.

- Pension file
  Pension files may contain information on next of kin or the service man or woman's entire immediate family if they are married. Additional records may include medical, vital, letters written by the soldier and his family, enlistment, and discharge records.

- Burial file or IDPF
  These files were created upon a soldier's death to record how he or she died and where they were buried. These documents sometimes contain letters from the family; disinterment records; service records; detailed cause of death; and health or state of the body information.

- State Bonus Application files
  These records may contain next of kin information, amount paid to the soldier or beneficiary if he was deceased, addresses, and signatures.

Major Wars in U.S. History

Below are a few of the wars fought by U.S. military men and women. This list is by no means comprehensive. The dates of U.S. involvement and types of records you may find are listed with each war.

Revolutionary War (1775-1783)

- Pension file

Civil War (1861-1865)

- Enlistment papers
- Compiled military service record
- Discharge papers
- Pension file (Confederate pensions would have been filed through the state for which they served, not the U.S. federal government.)

World War I (1917-1918)

World War I raged from 1914-1918 but the U.S. did not officially join the fight until 1917.

- Enlistment papers
- Service records
- Discharge papers
- Pension file
- Burial file
- State Bonus Application files

World War II (1941-1945)

World War II raged from 1939 -1945 but the U.S. did not officially join the fight until late 1941 after the Japanese attacked Pearl Harbor.

- Enlistment papers
- Service records
- Discharge papers
- Pension file
- IDPF
- State Bonus Application files

Korean War (1950-1953)

- Enlistment papers
- Service records
- Discharge papers
- Pension file
- IDPF

Vietnam War (1960-1975)

- Enlistment papers
- Service records
- Discharge papers
- Pension file
- IDPF

Assignment

Part I: After reading the memoirs and diary in the reading assignment, pretend you were a Civil War soldier like Jefferson. Write your own diary entry about participating in the Civil War. This entry should be at least two pages long. You can consult other Civil War sources for additional information on the life of a soldier.

Resources:
The Civil War Homepage
http://www.civil-war.net/

Timeline of the Civil War from Library of Congress
http://memory.loc.gov/ammem/cwphtml/tl1861.html

Sergeant Henry W. Tisdale
http://civilwardiary.net/

Part II: Visit Fold3.com http://fold3.com and register for a free 7-day trial so you can access military records.

Sign on and click "Records" and "List All Records." Scroll down to "Civil War Service Records."

Select "Confederate Records." Search for "Shannon, Pleasant."

Pleasant Shannon served as a Private in Co. I, Newton's Regiment (2nd Regiment Arkansas Cavalry) in Arkansas. He may also appear in records as Shannon, P M.

Part III: Read through his Compiled Military Service Records on Fold3.com. Write a one-page report about their contents.

Lesson 21: Religious and Cemetery Records

Goal

Learn the value of church and cemetery records and where to locate them.

Vocabulary

Baptismal Records: Written facts and documents about the baptism of an individual.

Cemetery: Land set aside for the burial of deceased persons.

Confirmation Records: Written facts and documents about the confirmation of an individual.

Grave: Location in a cemetery where a deceased person is buried.

Tombstone: A stone placed on the grave that provides information about the deceased.

Reading Assignment

Croom, Emily Anne. *The Genealogist's Companion and Sourcebook.* Cincinnati: Betterway Books, 2003.
> Read Chapter 4, pages 120-140

Lesson

Religious Records

Religious records may hold clues to familial relationships, but where can you find the possible religious affiliations of your ancestors?

- Probate records
- Marriage records
- Family stories
- Family Bible
- Census records or city directories – occupation notes

- Death certificates
- News articles
- Obituaries
- Family interviews

If you know the religious affiliation of your ancestors, where can you find out where religious records held? Contact the local church or parish where your ancestor attended. Some records will be held at the church or parish office. In some cases, an area's

© 2018 Jennifer Holik World War II Research & Writing Center

records may be held in an archive. For example, the Chicago area Catholic Church records are held at the Archdiocese Office in Chicago rather than at the individual churches.

What types of records may be held by a religious organization?

- **Baptismal Records**
  These records may contain the full name of the individual being baptized, names of the parents and godparents, date of birth, and baptismal date. If the church asked the parents and godparents to attend a class to prepare them for the baptism there may be additional information on file.

- **Confirmation Records**
  These records may contain the full name of the individual being confirmed and possibly his confirmation name. Names of his parents, sponsor, baptismal date, and other information may be available.

- **Marriage Records**
  Religious organizations may have kept a register of those married in the church and the name of the religious leader who performed the ceremony. There may have also been additional information recorded on a certificate or in a marriage file for the couple. If the organization required the couple to attend a pre-marriage class, additional information may be available.

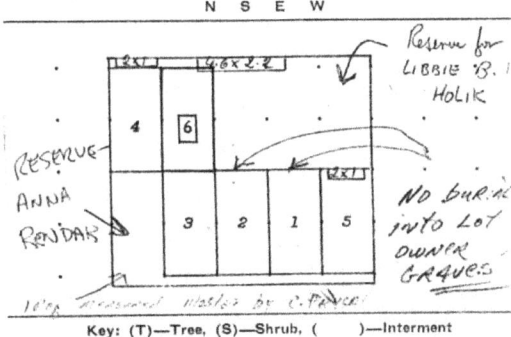

Cemetery Records

A **cemetery** is where we find our deceased ancestors. Records held by a religious organization or cemetery office can help prove genealogical relationships. In addition to the records shown below, cemeteries may have drawings of the tombstones, death certificates, obituaries, and other papers in the decedent's file. Each cemetery is different so always check to see what they hold.

Source: "Bohemian National Cemetery Plot Ownership Cards" (plot ownership files, n.d., Bohemian National Cemetery), plot owned by John Holik.

The cemetery plot card to the right lists the interment numbers, names, ages, interment dates, and sometimes the type of container for each person buried in the plot. The card also shows a drawing of the grave locations within the plot.

The people buried in this plot are relatives of the author. Marie Holik and John Holik are the author's great grandparents. They are buried with some of their children.

It is important to remember that just as other documents may contain errors, so can cemetery records.

Tombstones may reveal a lot about a person or persons buried in a grave. Names, birth and death dates, relationships, and photographs may provide information we did not have previously. This stone contains information on four individuals: Fortunato Fratto, Filomena Fratto, Florence Tellerino, and Teresa Iozzo.

What information does the stone contain for each individual? How does this information help your genealogical research? From the age of Fortunato and Filomena, can you calculate an approximate year of birth?

Source: Fratto Grave; grave photograph, privately held by Jennifer Holik [ADDRES FOR PRIVATE USE] Woodridge, Illinois, 2012.

Source: Fortunato Fratto Grave; grave photograph, privately held by Jennifer Holik [ADDRES FOR PRIVATE USE] Woodridge, Illinois, 2012.

What big clue does this photograph of Fortunato Fratto provide?

Photographs found on tombstones are sometimes the only photographs we can find of our ancestors. Always take several pictures of the tombstone and photographs and details of the stone for your records.

Explore the tombstones of those buried around your relatives. You may discover additional family members nearby that were not buried in the plot for which you were looking.

Assignment

Part I: Visit a cemetery where your family is buried. Talk to the cemetery office about obtaining records and plot maps. Walk the cemetery and photograph the graves. Write a brief report about your cemetery visit.

Part II: Visit one of these free websites and search for your ancestors.

Billion Graves
http://billiongraves.com

FindAGrave.com
http://findagrave.com

Lesson 22: Immigration

Goal

Understand what immigration means and how to locate records for your ancestors.

Vocabulary

Immigrant: An individual who comes from one place to another for the purpose of temporary or permanent residence.

Immigration: To enter a place from another for the purpose of temporary or permanent residence.

Port of Entry: The port or city where a ship docked and immigrants entered the United States.

Ship Manifest (Passenger List): A list of passengers on a ship.

Steerage: The lowest part of the ship where tickets were least expensive.

Reading Assignment

Croom, Emily Anne. *The Genealogist's Companion and Sourcebook.* Cincinnati: Betterway Books, 2003.
    Read Immigration and Naturalization pgs. 387-406.

Ellis Island's "History"
http://www.ellisisland.org/genealogy/ellis_island_history.asp

Lesson

The United States has been described as a melting pot because of all the different nationalities that immigrated and make up our nation's people. But where did the **immigrants** come from? How did they get here? What records show their arrival?

Immigration statistics will show that the highest immigration to the United States occurred between the years 1880 and 1930. You can view this and other information on Ellis Island's "The Peopling of America" page here:
http://www.ellisisland.org/immexp/wseix_4_3.asp?MID=00122907020054445888&
By clicking a time period you can see approximately how many people of each nationality entered the United States.

The reasons our ancestors left their homelands to come to the United States vary. Many of the reasons revolved around hunger, poverty, constant war, discrimination in the form of language, religion, ethnicity, and culture. Many came here for a better life because what they were leaving behind was so horrible.

Our ancestors may have come to the United States alone or as part of a family group. Sometimes the men in the family would come first to start a life and earn money. They would then send for part or all of the rest of their family, so the family came in waves to the United States.

Consider for a moment what it would be like to have your father leave the family to move across the ocean and not return. Perhaps you will wait a year or two or more before you are on a ship crossing that same ocean to meet him. What do you think that would feel like? What do you think it would feel like to leave your grandparents and cousins behind with the possibility that you will never see them again?

Our ancestors boarded ships to bring them from their countries in Europe or elsewhere to the United States. In the 1700s and 1800s, that journey might have taken months. By the late 1800s and early 1900s, the journey may have taken weeks. As ships were better designed and made to sail faster, the journey turned into days.

On the ships, many immigrants traveled in **steerage** unless they could afford first class tickets. On most ships immigrants were crammed in as tight as they could be packed. The voyage was often rough and people were sick, yet there was nowhere to go. Once they reached their **port of entry**, relief likely washed over them as the worst of the journey was over.

After arriving at the port of entry, the **ship manifest** would be presented and immigrants processed. The most famous port of entry was Ellis Island in New York which became active in 1892. This large processing station required passengers be examined to ensure no one entered the country that would become a burden on society, transfer a contagious disease, or arrive penniless. Those convicted of a crime were often turned away. Those deemed unfit to enter the country were sent home on the next available steamship.

Many of the ship manifests still exist today and can be found in the National Archives and various places online such as Ancestry.com and Ellis Island.org. Searching these manifests will help you locate information on your immigrant ancestor. Manifests may include, in addition to the name, age, occupation, and country of origin, the following:

- Physical description
- Name and address of nearest family member in the old country

- Name and address of family member they are meeting in the United States
- Amount of money they were carrying.

The information provided depends on the time of immigration. Manifests contained a great deal more information after 1906.

Ship manifests may help you uncover additional family members and information about individuals you currently have in your family tree. It is important to note that names were not always spelled correctly. When you search the indexes for your ancestor, look for other spellings. In addition, not all ship manifests survived so there may be times you cannot locate a manifest for a relative.

Discussion

1. Ask the student what they think it might be like to travel over the ocean for a week or a month.

2. Ask the student what they might bring with them if they were immigrating.

3. Many families are still immigrating to the United States but not coming by ship. Instead they come by plane or car. Discuss how this is different than the way our ancestors immigrated.
Follow the steps to locate a ship manifest.

Assignment

Part I: Learn more about Ellis Island by taking a tour. Listen to the audio recording, view the photo, and video available on each page of the tour.
http://teacher.scholastic.com/activities/immigration/tour/index.htm

Answer the following questions.

1. How many immigrants passed through Ellis Island?

2. Who was the first immigrant to arrive on Ellis Island when it reopened in 1900?

3. As immigrants ascended the stairs to the great hall, how many different chalk marks could a doctor use to identify an illness or issue with an immigrant?

4. View the medical chart on Stop 3: The Great Hall. What did the chalk marks identify? Name them.

5. How long did immigrants remain on Ellis Island?

6. Explain the literacy test.

7. In 1909, how much money was an immigrant required to have before they were allowed to enter the United States?

8. What two places did the ferry boats take processed immigrants?

Part II: Read the story of an immigrant child.
http://teacher.scholastic.com/activities/immigration/seymour/index.htm

Write a one-page report highlighting the life of Seymour Rechtzeit

Part III: Follow the steps to locate a ship manifest.

1. Visit Ellis Island.org at http://ellisisland.org

2. Conduct a basic passenger search for the surname **HOLIK**. View the results.

3. Now click "Refine Search" at the top of the page. On this screen in the field for "Name of Town/Village of Origin" type in **SENETIN**. Click search.

4. View the ship manifest for the person that appears.

5. Write a brief report about the information you found on the ship manifest.

Optional
Search Ellis Island for ancestors in your family who may have immigrated.

Lesson 23: Naturalization Records

Goal

To learn the reason for naturalization records and understand the information they may contain.

Vocabulary

Declaration of Intention: A sworn statement, given in court, made by an alien in which he announces his intent to become a citizen of the United States.

Naturalization: A sworn statement, given in court, made by an alien in which he renounces his allegiance to his country of origin and swears allegiance to the United States.

Petition for Naturalization: A document filed after a Declaration of Intention, by the immigrant, declaring their desire to become an official citizen.

Ship Manifest (Passenger List): An official list of all individual's on a given voyage. Information may include name; age; occupation; relative's information; country of origin; town of origin; and physical description.

Reading Assignment

Congress for Kids "Citizenship" section
http://www.congressforkids.net/citizenship_1_whatis.htm

Lesson

Continuing on an ancestor's journey, after immigration may have come naturalization. The reading you did for Lesson 22 also applies to this lesson. If an ancestor did not immigrate, there will be no naturalization papers unless they married an immigrant at a time when the laws changed. For a period of time between the years 1907 and 1922, if a U.S. born woman married an immigrant (alien), she would lose her citizenship.

Once an immigrant arrived in the United States, after a period of time, they were allowed to apply for citizenship. The amount of time required for an immigrant to live in the country depended on the time period.

The first step toward **naturalization** was declaring the intention to become a citizen. Immigrants or the courts would complete a **Declaration of Intention** which stated the country from which the immigrant had come and was giving up their allegiance. Early Declaration of Intentions had very little information but as time passed and the 1900s arrived, the forms became more detailed.

The second step toward naturalization was to file a **Petition for Naturalization**. Again, a certain amount of time had to pass before this could be filed. The time was determined by immigration laws. This document also contained the final oath where the immigrant swore allegiance to the United States. Petitions for Naturalizations after 1900 contained a great deal of information about the immigrant and, often, his family. Depending on the time period, a child who immigrated with his parents was also naturalized when the father swore his oath.

Naturalization papers can be found today in the National Archives, local and state archives, and county court archives. In addition to examining the information about your ancestor, pay special attention to the witnesses. Witnesses were often friends, family, or neighbors. Through these collaterals, you may discover additional information on your family. These documents, gathered with ship manifests, can provide invaluable evidence about your family.

Assignment

Part I: At the bottom of each section of the Congress for Kids "Citizenship" area there are Word Plays and Worksheets. Complete each as you read through the reading assignment.

Part II: Examine the following sets of naturalization records. Write a brief report containing the following:

- Dates of each set of papers
- Main pieces of information included in each set of papers
- How each set of papers differ
- Explain why the last set of papers may be the most helpful with your research

Review Frank Holik's papers that follow.

Optional: The Congress for Kids website has multiple sections on being a good citizen. They include: Attitudes & Actions, Responsible Citizenship, Communicating, Keeping Freedom, and What Do You Think. Read the remaining areas and complete the Word Plays and Worksheets within each section.

Additional Resources

Congress for Kids website
http://www.congressforkids.net/index.htm
This website not only discusses citizenship but also history of the United States and branches of the government.

No. 109427

UNITED STATES OF AMERICA

DECLARATION OF INTENTION
(Invalid for all purposes seven years after the date hereof)

UNITED STATES OF AMERICA	In the .... DISTRICT .... Court
NORTHERN DISTRICT OF ILLINOIS	of THE UNITED STATES of CHICAGO, ILLINOIS

I, FRANK HOLIK

now residing at 3520 S. 53rd Ct., Cicero, Cook Illinois

occupation Foreman, aged 45 years, do declare on oath that my personal description is:
Sex Male color White, complexion Dark color of eyes Dark Brown
color of hair Black, height 5 feet 5 inches; weight 198 pounds; visible distinctive marks None

race Bohemian; nationality Czecho-Slovakian
I was born in Senetin, Czecho-Slovakia, on November 35, 1890
I am married. The name of my wife or husband is Agnes
we were married on March 13, 1911, at Chicago, Illinois; she or he was
born at Kraselof, Czecho-Slovakia on March 27, 1888 entered the United States
at New York, New York, on May 1, 1906, for permanent residence therein, and now
resides at Cicero, Illinois I have Four children, and the name, date and place of birth,
and place of residence of each of said children are as follows:

Sylvia, born Sept. 16, 1913 in Chicago, resides in Cicero
Frank " Oct. 17, 1916 " " " " " " "
Anna " March 20, 1919 " " " " " " "
Vlasta " August 23, 1933 " Cicero " " "

I have not heretofore made a declaration of intention: Number ....

my last foreign residence was Senetin, Czecho-Slovakia
I emigrated to the United States of America from Rotterdam, Holland
my lawful entry for permanent residence in the United States was at New York, New York
under the name of Holik, Franoisek, on March 15, 1910
on the vessel SS Ryndam

I will, before being admitted to citizenship, renounce forever all allegiance and fidelity to any foreign prince, potentate, state, or sovereignty, and particularly, by name, to the prince, potentate, state, or sovereignty of which I may be at the time of admission a citizen or subject; I am not an anarchist; I am not a polygamist nor a believer in the practice of polygamy; and it is my intention in good faith to become a citizen of the United States of America and to reside permanently therein; and I certify that the photograph affixed to the duplicate and triplicate hereof is a likeness of me; So HELP ME GOD.

[signature]

Subscribed and sworn to before me in the office of the Clerk of said Court,
at Chicago, Illinois this 25th day of February
anno Domini 19 36 Certification No. 11-126630 from the Commissioner of Immigration and Naturalization showing the lawful entry of the declarant for permanent residence on the date stated above, has been received by me. The photograph affixed to the duplicate and triplicate hereof is a likeness of the declarant.

HENRY W. FREEMAN

[SEAL] Clerk of the U. S. DISTRICT Court.
by [signature] Deputy Clerk.

Form 2202-L-A
U. S. DEPARTMENT OF LABOR
IMMIGRATION AND NATURALIZATION SERVICE

No. 53697

Source: Declaration of Intention, 109427, Holik, Frank, February 25, 1936; U.S. District Court for the Northern District of Illinois; Records of District Courts of the United States, Record Group 21; National Archives and Records Administration– Great Lakes Region (Chicago).

ORIGINAL
(To be retained by clerk)

UNITED STATES OF AMERICA

198

PETITION FOR NATURALIZATION   No.

To the Honorable the _____ District _____ Court of _____ the United States _____ at _____ Chicago, Illinois _____

The petition of _____ FRANK HOLIK _____, hereby filed, respectfully shews:

(1) My place of residence is 3620 S. 53rd Court, Cicero, Ill. (2) My occupation is Foreman & truck driver

(3) I was born in Sonetin, Czechoslovakia on Nov. 25, 1890. My race is Bohemian

(4) I declared my intention to become a citizen of the United States on February 25, 1936 in the District

Court of _____ the United States _____ at _____ Chicago, Illinois _____

(5) I am married. The name of my wife is Agnes

we were married on March 13, 1911 at Chicago, Illinois she was

born at Kraselof, Czechoslovakia on March 27, 1888 entered the United States

at New York, N. Y. on May 1, 1908 for permanent residence therein, and now

resides at Cicero, Illinois I have 4 children, and the name, date,

and place of birth, and place of residence of each of said children are as follows:

Sylvia, born Sept. 13, 1913, in Chicago, Ill., now resides in Cicero, Illinois

Frank, " Oct. 17, 1916, " " " " " " " " " "

Anna,   " Mar. 20, 1919, " " " " " " " " " "

Vlasta, " Aug. 23, 1923, " " " " " " " " " "

(6) My last foreign residence was Sonetin, Czechoslovakia I emigrated to the United States of

America from Rotterdam, Holland My lawful entry for permanent residence in the United States

was at New York, N. Y. under the name of Holik, Francisek

on March 15, 1910 on the vessel Ryndam

as shown by the certificate of my arrival attached hereto.

(7) I am not a disbeliever in or opposed to organized government or a member of or affiliated with any organization or body of persons teaching disbelief in or opposed to organized government. I am not a polygamist nor a believer in the practice of polygamy. I am attached to the principles of the Constitution of the United States and well disposed to the good order and happiness of the United States. It is my intention to become a citizen of the United States and to renounce absolutely and forever all allegiance and fidelity to any foreign prince, potentate, state, or sovereignty, and particularly to _____

THE CZECHOSLOVAK REPUBLIC

of whom (which) at this time I am a subject (or citizen), and it is my intention to reside permanently in the United States. (8) I am able to speak the English language. (9) I have resided continuously in the United States of America for the term of five years at least immediately preceding the date of this petition, to wit, since

March 15, 1910 and in the County of Cook, Illinois

this State, continuously next preceding the date of this petition, since March, 1910 being a residence within said county of at least six months next preceding the date of this petition.

(10) I have not heretofore made petition for Naturalization: Number _____ on _____

at _____ and such petition was denied by that Court for the following reasons and causes, to wit:

and the cause of such denial has since been cured or removed.

Attached hereto and made a part of this, my petition for citizenship, are my declaration of intention to become a citizen of the United States, certificate from the Department of Labor of my said arrival, and the affidavits of the two verifying witnesses required by law.

Wherefore, I, your petitioner, pray that I may be admitted a citizen of the United States of America.

I, your aforesaid petitioner being duly sworn, depose and say that I have read this petition and know the contents thereof; that the same is true of my own knowledge except as to matters herein stated to be alleged upon information and belief, and that as to those matters I believe it to be true; and that this petition is signed by me with my full, true name.

Frank Holik

(Complete and true signature of petitioner)

AFFIDAVITS OF WITNESSES

Frank F. Kucera _____, occupation Trucking business _____ and

residing at 2805 S. Harding Ave., Chicago, Illinois

Anton G. Bratyanski _____, occupation Clerk

residing at 3636 S. 53rd Court, Cicero, Illinois

each being severally, duly, and respectively sworn, deposes and says that he is a citizen of the United States of America; that he has personally known and has been acquainted in the United States with

FRANK HOLIK the petitioner above mentioned, since April 28, 1921

and that to his personal knowledge the petitioner has resided in the United States continuously preceding the date of filing this petition, of which this affidavit is a part, to wit, since the date last mentioned, and at Cicero, Illinois in the County of Cook

this State, in which the above-entitled petition is made, continuously since April 28, 1921 and that he has personal knowledge that the petitioner is and during all such periods has been a person of good moral character, attached to the principles of the Constitution of the United States, and well disposed to the good order and happiness of the United States, and that in his opinion the petitioner is in every way qualified to be admitted a citizen of the United States.

Frank F. Kucera   *Anton G. Bratyanski*

(Signature of witness)   (Signature of witness)

Subscribed and sworn to before me by the above-named petitioner and witnesses in the office of the Clerk of said Court at Chicago, Ill.

this 28th day of April Anno Domini 1938. I hereby certify that certificate of arrival No. 11-126650

from the Department of Labor, showing the lawful entry for permanent residence of the petitioner above named, together with declaration of intention No.

109427 of such petitioner, has been by me filed with, attached to, and made a part of this petition on this date.

HENRY M. FRERMAN _____ Clerk.

Marjorie Schoenman (SEAL)

Deputy Clerk.

GW

Source: Petition, 198, Holik, Frank, April 28, 1938; U.S. District Court for the Northern District of Illinois; Records of District Courts of the United States, Record Group 21; National Archives and Records Administration– Great Lakes Region (Chicago).

OATH OF ALLEGIANCE

I hereby declare, on oath, that I absolutely and entirely renounce and abjure all allegiance and fidelity to any foreign prince, potentate, state, or sovereignty, and particularly to....The Czechoslovak Republic.....................

....
of whom (which) I have heretofore been a subject (or citizen); that I will support and defend the Constitution and laws of the United States of America against all enemies, foreign and domestic; that I will bear true faith and allegiance to the same; and that I take this obligation freely without any mental reservation or purpose of evasion: SO HELP ME GOD. In acknowledgment whereof I have hereunto affixed my signature.

X *Frank Holik*
(signature of petitioner)

Sworn to in open court, this ....6th.... day of ....October.... A. D. 19.38

...., Clerk.

By..., Deputy Clerk.

NOTE.—In renunciation of title of nobility, add the following to the oath of allegiance before it is signed: "I further renounce the title of (give title or titles) an order of nobility, which I have heretofore held."

Petition granted: Line No. ...14... of List No. ..3147.. and Certificate No. ..4508955.. issued.

Petition denied: List No. ....

Petition continued from .... to .... Reason ....
14—2618

Source: Petition, 198, Holik, Frank, April 28, 1938; U.S. District Court for the Northern District of Illinois; Records of District Courts of the United States, Record Group 21; National Archives and Records Administration– Great Lakes Region (Chicago).

Lesson 24: Newspapers

Goal

Learn what resources newspapers hold for genealogists.

Vocabulary

Newspaper: Printed publication consisting of folded unstapled sheets. These sheets contain news articles, correspondence, weather, advertisements, obituaries, and travel information.

Obituary: Notice of the death and funeral of an individual in a newspaper.

Social Column: A column that records the comings and goings of people in the town or city; also records births, engagements, marriages, and deaths.

Lesson

A **newspaper** contains a lot of information. That information varies from paper to paper but will always contain the latest news, updates on news from prior days or weeks, weather, **obituaries**, advertisements, and sports. Older newspapers may also contain a **social column** of this family visiting someone in town or a couple's engagement or marriage.

Obituaries vary in their content but contain the name of the deceased and usually names of some of his family members. Military information is often included which provides clues as to where to obtain additional information. Other items may include residential address of the deceased, occupation, name of the funeral home and cemetery, and time of the wake and funeral.

Newspapers are printed daily in cities across the country. Many are now available online, but what about non-current newspapers? Many old newspapers are being microfilmed and stored in libraries, archives, and historical societies. Some of those newspapers are also being preserved online through sites such as *Newspaper Archive* or *ProQuest*. Many libraries offer newspaper databases as part of their services. You can access some of these from home. See if there are indexes or compilations of articles created by local genealogy societies or historical societies.

What newspaper databases does your library offer?

Examine newspapers whenever you search for family. You may be surprised at the amount of information that can be obtained.

Assignment

Visit the *Chicago Tribune* online at http://chicagotribune.com Locate the obituary section and look through some obituaries. Select one obituary and write it out on the worksheet on the next page. Answer the following questions.

Put on your detective hat and look for clues! Write the obituary and answer the questions below.

Obituary

1. What is the name of the deceased?

2. Did he serve in the military?

3. What was his date of death?

4. In what unit did he serve?

5. Are any of his family members named?

6. What are their names?

7. What other information can you pull from the obituary?

Lesson 25: Research Plans and Logs

Goal

Create a research plan for your genealogical research.

Vocabulary

Research Log: A worksheet that tracks the genealogical sources you have checked, where you found them, what your comments are about the source, and the information you discovered.

Research Plan: A plan you create to help you (possibly) solve a genealogical problem. Strategically outlines what you know, what you want to know, where you might be able to find it, and how you will go about implementing this plan.

Reading Assignment

How to Develop a Genealogy Research Plan from About.com
http://genealogy.about.com/od/basics/a/research_plan.htm

Lesson

Research plans are a must for every researcher regardless of age. The plans help keep us on track. They help us know what issues we have had and how we attacked them. They also serve as a refresher when we leave a problem for a while and then return to it.

Traditionally, research plans are plans only. For our purposes, there is a summary spot at the bottom of the research plan example form. Use this to record your thoughts about the information you located and did not locate. For example, maybe one item on your plan to search was the 1920 Census for a family. You did not find them even after a page-by-page search. This needs to be noted in your research summary.

In traditional genealogy, this summary would be written up in a research report where you basically state the problem, the plan, the analysis and the results followed by next steps. But for our purposes of an overview, simply write your summary on your research plan.

Research logs are forms that help us plan our research trip and help us keep track of sources we viewed. Logs can be used in a couple of ways. First, take blank forms with you to the repository or library. Fill them out as you research. Second, fill in part of a research log with the sources you know you want to view. Take an extra form for additional items you may discover while you are researching.

The basic function of both forms is to help organize you, your research, and your results. It is a good idea to begin using these at the start of your research rather than wait until you have years of work behind you.

Discuss, with the student, a problem you would like to solve. Your discussion may go something like the following:

Teacher/Parent: *What would you like to find out about your family or [insert specific person's name]?*
Child answers

Teacher/Parent: *Ok, what do we know about your great-grandpa John?*
Help walk the student through what you know from the pedigree chart, family group sheet, and any records or photographs you have. Help them write down what they already know.

Teacher/Parent: *What do you think the answer is?*
This may be a difficult concept for younger children so help them out with this one.

Teacher/Parent: *Now where do you think we can find the answer to this question?*
Give the student a couple of ideas. If it is a census question, then use the U.S. Federal Census. If they are looking for the birthdate of someone, then possible answers may be U.S. Federal Census, birth certificates, death certificates, or gravestones.

Teacher/Parent: *What do you think we should do first to try to find the answer?*
Give the student three suggestions to help them put the suggestions in order. Sometimes there is no one right way to organize research.

Example Problem and Research Plan: Maybe that problem is to find out where the child's great grandparents lived in 1930. A research plan for this type of problem might look something like this:

Goal(s) or question(s) to answer: Find great-grandpa Frank Murabito and great-grandma Theresa nee Fratto, Murabito on the 1930 Census.
What is it I want to know?

Facts known: Frank Murabito was born in 1899 in Italy. His parents were born in Italy. Theresa Murabito was born in 1900 in Illinois. Her parents were born in Italy. They

married in Chicago, Illinois in 1919. Frank and Theresa Murabito were living at 1234 Alphabet Street, Chicago, Illinois on the 1920 Census.
List of all the facts I found while I was researching.

Hypothesis: Frank and Theresa Murabito probably live alone, meaning not with either set of parents since they are married. Or, Frank and Theresa Murabito are living with one of the parents.
Say what you think the research will tell you.

Possible sources: 1930 U.S. Federal Census records.
List where you may find this information.

Research plan: To search the 1930 U.S. Federal Census to locate Frank and Theresa Murabito in 1930.

Assignment

Part I: Choose a research problem you are having or identify something you want to know about an individual or family. Make sure this is something you could work on right now. Create a research plan to help you work through this problem or locate information.

Part II: Use the research plan you wrote with the research log, and try to solve your problem or locate the information you seek. Write a brief report about your process and results.

Additional Resources

Research Question File
http://www.byub.org/ancestors/charts/pdf/researchquestions.pdf

Example Research Plan

The research plan example provided below will hopefully give you a few ideas on how to write your own. There is no one correct way. You have to write your plan the way it makes sense to you.

RESEARCH PLAN

Goal(s) or Question(s) to Answer:

Facts Known:

Hypothesis:

Possible Sources:

Research Plan:

Example Research Log

Use this log to track your research or create your own log. Logs can be easily created in Excel to record information there or to print.

RESEARCH LOG

Ancestor's Name or Repository:

Objective(s):

Date of Search	Location/Call No.	Description of Source	Comments and Questions

Lesson 26: Timelines

Goal

Understand how timelines are helpful in genealogical research. Learn to create a timeline of your life.

Vocabulary

Timeline: The passage of time represented graphically.

Item Needed

Geneosity.com's Timeline Sheet

http://www.geneosity.com/genealogy-timeline-chart/

Reading Assignment

Using Timelines in Your Research by Donna Pzrecha on Genealogy.com

http://www.genealogy.com/36_donna.html

Lesson

A timeline is a drawing that helps us place information in the correct time period. This is typically designed in decade format or year-by-year depending on how long of a period you wish to capture.

Timelines can help us see when big events occurred in the lifetime of an ancestor or family. Not only can we capture big events in an individual's life but also capture local and world history events that were happening during that individual's lifetime. These events may lead us to new record sources which will help us tell a fuller story of the lives of our ancestors.

To the parent/teacher: Print and discuss the timelines listed above in the Items Needed section. Use your life as an example, and complete one timeline with your child/students so they have a greater understanding of the concept. Read through the assigned reading for another example of how to use timelines.

Younger students can create timelines that capture the important events in their life. Some examples are:

- Birth of individual or student
- Births of siblings
- Important things to them such as vacations, the year they lost their first tooth, when they started preschool or kindergarten, the death of a grandparent, etc.

Example 1

2 0 0 5	2 0 0 6	2 0 0 7	2 0 0 8	2 0 0 9	2 0 1 0	2 0 1 1	2 0 1 2

Birth   Disney   Preschool   Disney World   Kindergarten
Today
               Cruise   Disney World

Example 2

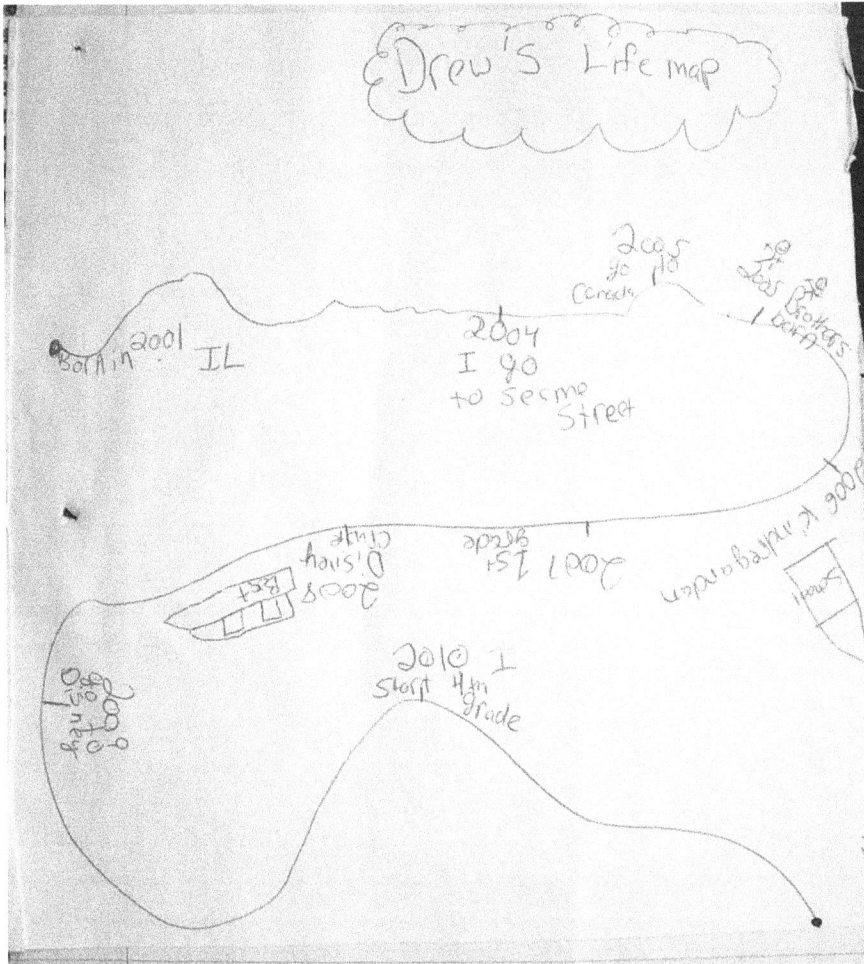

Example of a life map by the author's son. Created in 4th grade in 2010-2011.

A life map is another form of a timeline. The student can draw their life's road and indicate important stops along the way. These important stops can be big events from their life and may also include historical events.

Assignment

Choose one option based on the age of your student(s).

Option 1: Create a timeline of the student's life. Include major events in their lives and things they consider to be important.

Create the timeline on a piece of paper (8.5x11) in landscape format.

Draw a line down the middle of the page to allow for years to be written above the line and information below the line. Encourage children to add pictures or drawings near the year or information to illustrate the event.

Option 2: Have the student complete one of the two timeline sheets printed from either Geneosity.com or PBS Ancestors.

Option 3: Create a life map.

Lesson 27: Examine it Once, Twice, and Again

Goal

Understand documents, research reports, books, and the like must be read more than once to fully grasp every piece of evidence provided. Reviewing these items and your work from time to time may yield new clues and realizations about your family history.

Assignment

Search Ancestry.com for Charlie Murabito's Draft Registration Card. Then, answer the questions on the worksheet on the next page.

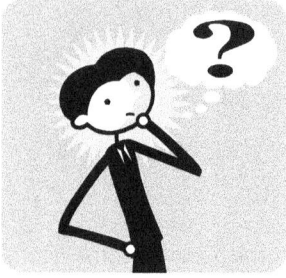

Some details in a document jump out at us right away while others do not.

1. What is the name of the registrant?

2. What was his occupation?

3. Where did he live?

4. How old was he?

Now look through the certificate again. What other details can you find?

1. What was his date of birth?

2. Who was his nearest relative and where did she live?

3. What date did he register for the draft?

Are there any other details you think are important from this document?

Lesson 28: Travel

Goal

Plan a family history research trip that is organized

Vocabulary

Repository: A place or building where things are or may be stored

Items Needed

Atlas

MapQuest.com   http://mapquest.com

Lesson

Written by Guest Contributor Terri O'Connell

Planning a research trip can be a fun activity for the family. Trips are a good teaching tool when it comes to explaining to children about the areas from which their family came. Students also use mapping and math skills.

To have a well-planned research trip, one must first decide in which area they want to research and second, what records are available in that area. Places you might look for records are: genealogy libraries, cemeteries, archives, churches, and courthouses. Always call ahead before visiting any repository or library to check on hours and inquire about the records you seek. In some cases, materials may need to be pulled prior to your visit.

While compiling this list of potential repositories to visit, it is imperative to keep track of all information for each location. This would include, the name of repository, address, phone number, contact name, hours of operation, what their collection holds, security policy, and photocopy fees. Create a spreadsheet that keeps all of this information together. It will make visiting the repositories easier.

Looking beyond repositories and cemeteries, there are other places you might want to consider seeing on a research trip. These include your ancestors' prior work locations, residences, and churches. These places are great photography opportunities for your family. Also, consider bringing a video camera and creating a video of the places that are personal to your family. One of your parents or siblings can video you as you play the reporter on the scene giving the camera all the information about the location and the ancestors who once lived there.

Assignment

Create a research trip.

Part I: Explore the areas in which your ancestors lived. What repositories and libraries are in that area? Create a list that includes the name of the repository and its address.

Part II: Use Mapquest.com to create a map of repositories you would like to visit. Add all of the above locations one at a time to create your map.

Lesson 29: Organizing Paper and Digital Files

Goal

Understand how to handle and care for the material you acquire while researching your family history.

Vocabulary

Clipping: A piece cut from a newspaper or magazine.

Document: A written or printed work that can be used as evidence or proof.

Ephemera: Mementos or souvenirs.

Photograph: An image made using a camera.

Scrapbook: A blank book in which documents, photographs, clippings, and ephemera are combined.

Stable: To keep something safe and secure to prevent it from being damaged or destroyed.

Reading Assignment

Read the American Association for State and Local History Technical Leaflet
http://www.msa.md.gov/msa/refserv/pdf/aaslh.pdf

Lesson – Paper Files

Written by Guest Contributor Laura Cosgrove Lorenzana

To the parent/teacher: This lesson is more advanced. Please read through it and adapt as needed for the age group you are teaching. The basic idea is to discuss ways to organize and store materials you locate as you continue researching.

Throughout these lessons you've found, received, or acquired many different types of material. Documents, photographs, clippings, and ephemera are all part of a family history collection. Because we work so hard to research and collect these items, they should be organized, cared for, and kept stable so they last a very long time. The first step is to learn the basic ideas for care and handling. The second step is to understand the best place to store the material. The third step is to organize and store these materials.

For the purposes of these lessons, much of what you've gathered and/or created is being stored in a binder. There are different types of plastic, some of which are not intended for long-term storage of paper material. Plastic is often produced with additives that actually cause harm to paper and photographs. Purchase plastic that is either polypropylene or mylar to ensure long term protection for the material.

Materials you wish to store flat can be stored using acid-free folders and boxes. These storage materials can be purchased from most office supply stores or through archival companies such as Hollinger Metal online. Acid-free containers help keep the paper chemically stable.

Care and Handling

What is the best way to handle the material that you've gathered? Wash your hands with plain soap and warm water before sitting down with your material. This is important because your hands naturally have oils in them. These oils, when transferred to the paper can cause it to deteriorate and/or hold dirt. When handling photographs, make certain to hold them on the edges, or if you can, wear white cotton gloves. You'll often see workers in museums and archives wearing gloves when they're handling material.

When picking up a document, always support it from the back. If you have documents, like old letters, that are folded, it's best to gently unfold them, put them between two pieces of acid-free paper and either put them in a mylar protector or an acid-free folder. The act of folding and unfolding a document breaks down the paper, and, if it's done too much, will eventually tear apart the paper.

Documents should not be stored with paper clips, staples, binder clips, or post-it notes. The metal in the clips can rust or tear the paper. There are chemicals in the adhesive in the post-it notes that is very harmful to paper and can either discolor it or cause it to degrade.

By handling your materials with care and storing them in a comfortable location, they will last for many years.

Storage of Materials

Documents and photographs on paper need to be protected from a variety of things that can harm them. Simple things like temperature, humidity, light, and pests can greatly affect how long paper lasts.

The key to long term storage of family history is A KIC! <u>A</u>lways <u>K</u>eep <u>I</u>t <u>C</u>omfortable. Materials need to be stored somewhere that *you* would be comfortable. Are you comfortable when it is really hot or really cold or when the temperature varies a lot? What about if it's very humid or very dry?

Remember to give your material AKIC:

The temperature should be between 60-70° Fahrenheit (15-21° Celsius) and the Relative Humidity between 40-50%. Why are temperature and humidity important? If the humidity is too low, the paper can become very dry and brittle causing it to fall apart when it's handled. If the humidity is too high, the material becomes damp which increases the chances for mold to grow. Mold is very bad as it quickly spreads and destroys paper.

There should be plenty of air movement.

Direct sunlight can cause fading, so keeping materials out the sun is also suggested.

Material should be kept in a place where there aren't any creepy, crawlies; no spiders, roaches, centipedes, mice, etc. Why is this important? Well, other than the gross factor, bugs and rodents carry dirt and bacteria on their bodies that when passed onto the paper can cause it to deteriorate. Many pests eat paper or use it to make nests.

Organization of Materials
Every person adjusts how they label and organize their material in their own way; however, these guidelines should assist you in creating a solid foundation on which to build your collection. Organizing your material is important for several reasons. It helps to ensure that you can easily find something when you need it, that you don't have to handle the material you have over and over as you look for something, and that the material you have is safe and stable.

Think of the organization of your paper files the same way you would your digital files. You can use either archival quality polypropylene enclosures in a binder or acid-free folders that can be stored in an archival box. In either case, organizing material by surname generally works best. Folders should be labeled using pencil. Why pencil? Getting in the habit of using pencil when working with your material is best because pens, markers, and other materials like that are permanent. Should they break or spill, they can permanently harm your paper and/or photographs. So, take care and use pencil.

Labels can be as simple as just the surname (i.e., Jones); however, as your collection grows, you may want to separate each person into their own folder/protector. In that case, the label should include the surname, give name, and a range of dates. The range of dates helps to keep individuals with the same name (Jones, John) separate. You can also add other identifying information on the outside of the folder, such as spouse (husband or wife), children, or where the person is buried. The folders can then be stored in alphabetical order by surname, then given name and, if you'd like, by the range of dates.

Lesson – Digital Files

Many of the records we view and use today are initially found online in digital format. We print and save these files throughout the course of our research, but do we have a way to organize and store them so they are easily located later? Digital files require just as much care in organization as your paper files. Here are some suggested steps to organize your digital files.

Step 1
Create a folder in your "My Documents" folder for "Genealogy."

Step 2
Create new folders within the "Genealogy" folder for each surname in your pedigree tree.

Step 3
Move the files you have downloaded into the appropriate surname folder.

Optional
To maintain more order when many records are downloaded and saved to your computer, consider creating folders within each surname for each record type, i.e. census, immigration, naturalization, military, and vital records.

Digital Organizational Resource
Sort Your Story   http://sortyourstory.com

Sort Your Story is a software program that allows you to create family files in which you can organize photos and documents for individuals in your family. This very visual program helps any level of researcher organize their files but it is particularly helpful to children and young adults. Organizing your records and notes in Sort Your Story helps you identify gaps in your research and build a more complete family history.

Assignment

Part I: Organize your paper files using the system outlined in the lesson.

Part II: Organize your digital files using the system outlined in the lesson.

Optional: Locate a suitable space in your home to store your family history collection. Remember to give the material A <u>K</u> <u>I</u> <u>C</u>. Closets are excellent spaces for keeping material stable. Space can often be made on a shelf, which is better than the floor. Or, if you have desk space or a desk drawer these would work as well. Don't forget to add your family history collection to your family's emergency plan too!

Additional Resources

Caring for Your Family Archives
The U.S. National Archives website has many resources for preserving family papers and memorabilia.
http://www.archives.gov/preservation/family-archives/

The Northeast Document Conservation Center (NEDCC.) A nonprofit, regional conservation center specializing in the preservation of paper-based materials. NEDCC serves libraries, archives, museums, historical societies and other collections-holding institutions, as well as private collections.
http://www.nedcc.org/resources/family.php

Lesson 30: Putting it all Together

Goal

Write the beginnings of a family history starting with yourself and an ancestor using the materials you have discovered.

Vocabulary

Autobiography: A story about your life, written by you.

Biography: A story about someone's life written by someone else.

Final Project

Part I: Write a brief autobiography that describes your family and your life.

Include the following:
- Title page and name of author, date of autobiography
- Your full name and birth information
- Names of your parents and siblings
- Information about your parents and siblings
- Information about education, hobbies and activities
- Anything else interesting about you that you want people to know
- Photographs.

The total length of your autobiography should be two to four pages.

Part II: Write the biography of one of your ancestors. Include all the information you have discovered throughout this project for that ancestor and his or her family.

Include the following:
- Title page with the name of the author and date of biography
- Name of the ancestor and siblings and parents
- Vital information on each family member
- The story of the ancestor using the records you locate; cite your sources
- Social and local history to place the ancestor in proper historical context
- Photographs, maps and other items that will enhance the story.

The total length of biography should be 5-8 pages depending on how much information you have collected about this particular ancestor.

```
P T N A L P H C R A E S E R S Y S E K E
U A Z O Y H A A I V H S B T J R C N T P
E Z S S I I C O N I H Z A X A O R I K H
T E U S U T M R P P Z B S W U T A L V E
K F I S E W A M A K L D Q Q T I P E Z M
D O D U Y N A R I E S J F M O S B M Z E
E V A R G N H G G S T G Q B O O I L R
Z Q N B I O R E I I R E E B I P O T F A
K H T F T C F T R H M A R B O E K R H V
B C E O C P R T Z L L M N T G R C N K I
A S H U V W N R L I I J I T R N W F J C
T P T O M B S T O N E S U J A D Q B E Q
E B K F D G R U G Q Q Z T B P R P M E T
M N X X J V L F Y V I H Y Q H X E N N K
N A T U R A L I Z A T I O N Y T Y E E R
L P C I P A L P W F Z A W N E J M X C L
C L I P P I N G C Q R R V R L U F J W I
A W Z I H L F X Z K O Q Y P C H Z H G S
Q V H Y L C Y R A U T I B O P C X G V M
Y A H B H Q N M C L T X D L O Z P Q W Z
```

AUTOBIOGRAPHY
CEMETERY
CLIPPING
DOCUMENT
EPHEMERA
GRAVE
IMMIGRANT
IMMIGRATION
NATURALIZATION
OBITUARY

PASSENGER LIST
PHOTOGRAPH
REPOSITORY
RESEARCH
RESEARCH PLAN
SCRAPBOOK
SHIP MANIFEST
STABLE
TIMELINE
TOMBSTONE

Define the Words:

AUTOBIOGRAPHY:

CEMETERY:

CLIPPING:

DOCUMENT:

EPHEMERA:

GRAVE:

IMMIGRANT:

IMMIGRATION:

NATURALIZATION:

OBITUARY:

PASSENGER LIST:

PHOTOGRAPH:

REPOSITORY:

RESEARCH:

RESEARCH PLAN:

SCRAPBOOK:

SHIP MANIFEST:

STABLE:

TIMELINE:

TOMBSTONE:

Glossary

Affidavit: An oath made before any person who is authorized to record an oath.

Ancestors: A person from whom one is descended.

Artifacts: Memorabilia passed down through the generations.

Birth Certificate: An official document issued when a person is born.

Burial File: A file created on a military man or woman who dies while in service. This title was given to files created during World War I.

Census: An official count of a population which records specific details about individuals and families.

Citation: Bibliographic origin of evidence.

Collateral lines: A line of descent connecting persons who share a common ancestor. These individuals are related through an aunt, uncle, or cousin.

Death Certificate: An official document issued when a person dies.

Declaration of Intention: A sworn statement, given in court, made by an alien in which he announces his intent to become a citizen of the United States.

Deed: A written legal document that authorizes the transfer of property.

Derivative Source: Material that is manipulated through copying such as extracts, transcriptions, abstracts, translations, and authored works.

Descendants: Those living after a person who are in a direct line such as a son or daughter, grandson or granddaughter, etc.

Direct Evidence: Information relevant to genealogy research that seems to answer a specific question.

Draft: Selective requirement for service in the U.S. armed forces. This was for naturalized white or native born citizens, male, age twenty-one and older.

Enumeration: A numbered list of data.

Enumeration District: A geographic region defined as a tract, area, or district, in which a census is taken.

Evidence: Something that pertains to an issue in question.

Fact: Something that actually exists; truth; reality.

Family Group Sheet: A collection of names and facts about one family unit.

Family History: The research of past events relating to a family or families, written in a narrative form.

Genealogy: A study of the family. It identifies ancestors and their information.
Grantee: Purchaser of property.

Grantor: Seller of property.

Hidden Source: A source of information you might not automatically think of when you search for family records.

Historical Context: For family history, historical context is placing a person into a specific era or time period to view their lives and decisions based on the time in which they lived.

Home Source: A home source is any item or document that will provide facts on people in our family.

Immigrant: An individual who comes from one place to another for the purpose of temporary or permanent residence.

Immigration: To enter a place from another for the purpose of temporary or permanent residence.

Indirect Evidence: Information relevant to genealogy research that cannot answer a specific question without other evidence or records.

Individual Deceased Personnel Files (IDPF): A file created on a military man or woman who dies while in service. This title was given to files created during World War II to the present day.

Interment: The location where a person will be laid to rest or buried.

Intestate: When someone dies without a will.

Journal: A diary, notebook, or other book in which to record your thoughts.

Letters of Administration: Document issued by the probate court to an individual authorizing them to settle the estate of one who dies intestate.

Letters Testamentary: Document issued to the executor of an estate giving authority to settle the estate of one who died testate.

Maiden Name: A woman's surname, or last name, prior to marriage.

Map: Representation of an area of land or sea showing physical features such as cities, roads, mountains, etc.

Marriage License: An official document issued to a couple so they may be married.

Maternal: Related through the mother's line.

Memorabilia: Items collected and kept because of personal or historical significance.

Migration: The movement of individuals or families from one locale to another.

Military Records: A set of records compiled by the U.S. government regarding an individual's enlistment, service, and discharge from the armed forces.

Naturalization: A sworn statement, given in court, made by an alien in which he renounces his allegiance to his country of origin and swears allegiance to the United States.

Obituary: A notice of someone's death that usually contains a little biographical information about them.

Occupation: A job.

Original Source: Material that has been unaltered and remains in its original form.

Paternal: Related through the father's line.

Pedigree Chart: A chart outlining the ancestors of an individual.

Pension File: File containing documents pertaining to a set fee paid to a U.S. armed forces veteran for past service to the government. These records sometimes contain service information; birth, marriage, and death records; family information; and health information.

Primary Source: A piece of evidence from the past that was created during the event.

Probate: Legal process of settling an estate.

Proof: Evidence or argument establishing or helping to establish a fact or truth of a statement.

Proof of Heirship: Testimony documenting the relationships of heirs listed in a probate file to the deceased.

Secondary Source: Sources created after an event by people who do not have firsthand knowledge of the event.

Ship Manifest (Passenger List): An official list of all individuals on a given voyage. Information may include name; age; occupation; relative's information; country of origin; town of origin; and physical description.

Social History: The study of the everyday lives of ordinary people.

Source: People, documents, artifacts, and print or digital materials.

Special Collection: Collection of rare manuscripts, books, and other materials that is stored in special rooms to preserve the materials in a library or archive.

Tax Rolls/Records: Records held by the city and/or county and state which assess the taxes on real and personal property.

Testate: When someone dies with a will.

Timeline: The passage of time represented graphically.
Tradition: The handing down of statements, beliefs, legends, customs, information, etc., from generation to generation, especially by word of mouth or by practice.

Vital Records: Governmental records on life events such as birth certificates, marriage licenses, and death certificates.

Will: Document in which a Testator disburses his estate, both real and personal property.

Appendix A
Websites and Books

Websites and Books

There are numerous wonderful online and book resources and this list is by no means comprehensive. It is meant to serve as a starting point for your research.

Ancestry.com   http://www.ancestry.com
This site is a paid website which allows users to build and share their family trees; conduct online research in Census Records, Vital Records, Ship Manifests, Military Records and more. There are some free databases available to search. This website also has tips, forms, experts, and message boards. You can sign up for a free 14-day trial.

FamilySearch.org   http://familysearch.org
Free site with Census Records, Vital Records, Military Records and more.

Fold3.com   http://fold3.com
Subscription site focused on military records but also contains some newspapers, census records, and other items. Free trial period available.

Genealogy.com   http://www.genealogy.com
Free website with learning resources, courses, and examples for research.

GoogleBooks   http://books.google.com/
Search a surname, county, military unit and see what books are listed. There are some full version books available and others which have partial views. If you find a book in which you are interested, check with your local library to borrow it or request it through inter-library loan.

HistoryGeo.com   http://historygeo.com
Subscription site with land maps from all over the United States. Maps being added monthly. Free trial available.

The In-Depth Genealogist   www.theindepthgenealogist.com

The In-Depth Genealogist is a digital newsletter that contributes to the advancement of all genealogists.

As a free monthly digital newsletter providing articles and columns for the advancement of all genealogists, professional or hobbyist, we share our knowledge and experience in a friendly, approachable, and entertaining way. Get in-depth with us!
You can sign up for the newsletter at http/:bit.ly/INDEPTHGEN

Library of Congress   http://loc.gov

Free website containing vast resources for researchers such as photographs, videos, primary sources, books, periodicals, maps, and manuscripts.

MyHeritage.com   http://myheritage.com

Online family tree site that offers both free and subscription options. Share your family tree with family members, the world, or keep it private.

National Archives   http://www.archives.gov

The National Archives website has many searchable database, help areas, ways to order records and a calendar of classes and events.

BOOKS

Croom, Emily Anne. *The Genealogist's Companion and Sourcebook.* Cincinnati: Betterway Books, 2003.

Greene, Bob, Fulford, D.G. *To Our Children's Children.* Doubleday, 1998.

Greenwood, Val D. *The Researcher's Guide to American Genealogy.* Baltimore: Genealogical Publishing Company, 1990. Note: This is for the second edition. A third edition is available.

Hart, Cynthia. *The Oral History Workshop.* New York: Workman Publishing Company, 2009.

Hatcher, Patricia Law. *Producing a Quality Family History.* Salt Lake City: Ancestry, Inc. 1996.

Mills, Elizabeth Shown. *Evidence Explained Citing History Sources from Artifacts to Cyberspace.* Baltimore: Genealogical Publishing Company, 2009.

Pfeiffer, Laura Szucs. *Hidden Sources Family History in Unlikely Places.* Orem: Ancestry Publishing, 2000.

Rose, Christine. *Courthouse Research for Family Historians.* San Jose: CR Publications, 2004.

Sturdevant, Katherine Scott. *Bringing Your Family History to Life through social history.* Cincinnati: Betterway Books, 2000. **This book is out of print but can be found through libraries and used book stores.

Szucs, Loretto Dennis, and Luebking, Sandra Hargreaves, editors. *The Source A Guidebook to American Genealogy.* Provo: Ancestry Publishing, 2006.

Appendix B
Worksheets

Source Summary Sheet

Ancestor's Name or Repository:

Date of Search	Location/Call No.	Name of Source, Author, Publisher	Information Discovered

Home Sources Worksheet

Be a detective!

Use this worksheet to start thinking about home sources. Put on your detective hat and search your home for sources that may provide clues for genealogy research.

Birth
- ☐ Birth certificate
- ☐ Baby book
- ☐ Scrapbook
- ☐ Birth announcement
- ☐ Baptismal record
- ☐ Christening record

Marriage
- ☐ Marriage certificate
- ☐ Marriage announcement in newspaper
- ☐ Scrapbook
- ☐ Photographs
- ☐ Divorce papers

Death
- ☐ Death certificate
- ☐ Obituary
- ☐ Mass card
- ☐ Funeral program
- ☐ Gravestone
- ☐ Will

Family Information
- ☐ Bibles
- ☐ Letters and emails
- ☐ Journals and diaries

- ☐ Newspaper articles
- ☐ Certificates
- ☐ Scrapbooks
- ☐ Photographs

Immigration Information
- ☐ Ship manifests
- ☐ Naturalization certificates
- ☐ Passports
- ☐ Photographs

Military Information
- ☐ Scrapbooks
- ☐ Service records
- ☐ Discharge records
- ☐ Pension files
- ☐ Draft Registration Cards
- ☐ Newspaper articles
- ☐ Photographs
- ☐ Uniforms

School Information
- ☐ Scrapbooks
- ☐ Report Cards
- ☐ Certificates
- ☐ Artwork
- ☐ Yearbooks

Home Sources Word Search

```
U Q S Z N Y U H J S L B M I K
R Y D D L E O Y K U G I W N N
U J C I R M W E B E D B I T Y
J P M X E O P S N U S L V E M
J A I E Z N C E P F Q E Q R U
F Y D D N K A E A A A G E M G
Y R A T I L I M R E P W E E N
P H O T O G R A P H S E C N U
V Y L G C A R D S K Q D R T Y
V I Y P T P J S L A C Q U S P
C O T N J R E Y O W T H O R H
I C O A V J A Y O X Q N S Q H
X D B U L N C X Y U C Q U Q A
X G T E B H I S W S P L I R Z
R T E H M I X I D N S S A M H
```

BIBLE	CARDS	FAMILY	GENEALOGY	HOME
INTERMENT	MASS	MILITARY	NEWSPAPERS	PHOTOGRAPHS
RECORDS	SOURCE	VITAL		

Hidden Sources Worksheet

Be a detective!

Use this worksheet to start thinking about hidden sources. Put on your detective hat and search your home for sources that may provide clues for genealogy research.

- ☐ Artifacts
- ☐ Association records
- ☐ Books
- ☐ Cemetery records
- ☐ Diaries and journals
- ☐ Dictionaries
- ☐ Insurance records

- ☐ Jewelry
- ☐ Job records, resumes
- ☐ Land records
- ☐ Licenses
- ☐ Maps
- ☐ Medical records

- ☐ Orphan records
- ☐ Report cards
- ☐ Social Security records
- ☐ Tax records

Hidden Sources Word Search

```
V A Y T W O Y M Y B P A N Y Z
G D G V A R S G V D L L C R I
X P S G O I O Z B H B G E A L
O Y W T F L L R S R I S M N R
W B S U A A H I D D E N E O L
N I I E V V M V B T L Q T I A
H Y N T A R T I F A C T E T C
G E V Z U K Y R L J R B R C I
G B R Q I A E R Q Y W O Y I D
M T R B B C R Q L F A O M D E
R N T C O W W Y D E B K P E M
L A N R U O J I F O W S J U M
O Z D P Q M A C Z I A E V X P
M S R W Q R A P Y Z L G J J V
S G G Q Y C Y U S E D L K L J
```

ARTIFACT	BOOKS	CEMETERY	DIARY
DICTIONARY	FAMILY	GENEALOGY	HIDDEN
HISTORY	JEWELRY	JOURNAL	MEDICAL
MEMORABILIA	OBITUARY	RECORDS	

Story Worksheet

_____

_____

_____

_____

_____

_____

_____

_____

_____

_____

_____

_____

_____

_____

_____

_____

_____

_____

Story Worksheet

_____

_____

_____

_____

_____

_____

_____

_____

_____

_____

_____

_____

_____

_____

_____

_____

List questions you have after writing the story.

_____

_____

_____

_____

_____

_____

_____

_____

_____

List records you could search which may lead to some answers to your questions.

_____

_____

_____

_____

_____

_____

Worksheet – What is Genealogy, and Why Should I Care?

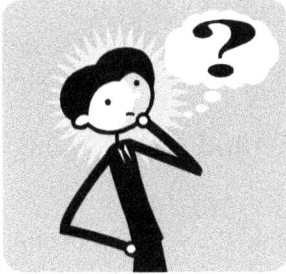

1. Why do I live where I live?

2. Which part of my family came to this place to settle down?

3. When did they come and why?

4. Some of our family members have light colored hair and eyes and others have darker colored skin and eyes. What is our background?

5. What jobs did my **ancestors** hold? Are they the same jobs my parents hold today?

6. Did my family move around a lot? Why?

7. How much education did my ancestors receive? Is it the same as what children receive today?

8. My mom makes special desserts or meals for the holidays. Where did those recipes come from? Why does she always make those same recipes year after year?

9. Where did our family **traditions** come from?

Family Interview Worksheet

Use this worksheet as a starting point to conduct your interview. Add more questions in the space provided.

1. What is your full name?

2. When and where were you born? What city and state? What hospital?

3. Who are your parents? When and where were they born? Are they married? When and where did they get married?

4. Did you have brothers and sisters? When and where were they born? Are they married? When and where did they get married? Do they have any kids? Who are they?

5. When you were growing up, where did you go to school? What were your favorite classes?

6. Did you go to college? What did you study?

7. What is your job?

8. Do you have a nickname?

9. Growing up did you live in a house or apartment?

10. What hobbies did you have as a kid? What hobbies do you have as an adult?

11. Did you get together with your aunts, uncles and cousins a lot growing up? If you did, what kinds of things did you do?

12. Why do I live where I live?

13. Did my family move around a lot? Why?

14. Which part of my family came to this place to settle down?

15. When did they come and why?

16. Where else did they settle?

17. Some of our family members have light colored hair and eyes and others have darker colored skin and eyes. What is our background?

18. How much education did my ancestors receive? Is it the same as what children receive today?

19. What jobs did my ancestors hold? Are they the same jobs my parents hold today?

20. What hobbies did my ancestors have? Were they in any clubs growing up or organizations as adults?

21. My mom makes special desserts or meals for holidays. Where did those recipes come from? Why does she always make those same recipes year after year?

22. What are our family traditions? Where did our family traditions come from?

23. _____ ?

24. _____ ?

25. _____ ?

26. _____ ?

27. _____ ?

28. _____ ?

29. _____ ?

30. _____ ?

Write down the date of your interview and the address where you are living. Keeping a log of addresses when you take interviews or find documents can help you locate new information.

Student Interview Worksheet

Use this worksheet as a starting point to conduct your interview. Add more questions in the space provided.

1. What is your full name?

2. When and where were you born? What city and state? What hospital?

3. Who are your parents? When and where were they born? Are they married? When and where did they get married?

4. Do you have brothers and sisters? When and where were they born?

5. Where do you go to school? What were your favorite classes?

6. What hobbies do you have?

7. _____ ?

8. _____ ?

9. _____ ?

10._____ ?

Scavenger Hunt

Examine examples of some commonly used documents in genealogical research. Write the answers to each question below.

World War I Draft Registration Card

1. What is the name of the individual?

2. What is his date of birth?

3. Where does he live?

4. What is their occupation and where do they work?

5. What other information on this document will help you piece together your family history?

Birth Certificate

1. What is the name of the child?

2. What are the names of his parents?

3. What other information on this certificate will help you piece together your family history?

Death Certificate

1. What is the name of the individual?

2. What are the names of his parents?

3. What other information on this certificate will help you piece together your family history?

Appendix C
Answer Key

Crossword Lessons 1 – 4

Across

3. GENEALOGY—A study of the family. It identifies ancestors and their information.
5. DESCENDANTS—Those living after a person who are in a direct line such as a son or daughter,
    grandson or granddaughter, etc.
7. COLLATERALLINES—A line of descent connecting persons who share a common ancestor. These
    individuals are related through an aunt, uncle, or cousin.
9. PUBLICHISTORY—Practicing history beyond a school environment in places such as historical
    museums or government agencies.
11. MATERNAL—Related through the mother's line.
12. FAMILYHISTORY—The research of past events relating to a family or families, written in a
    narrative form.
13. MAIDENNAME—A woman's surname, or last name, prior to marriage.

Down

1. FAMILYGROUPSHEET—A collection of names and facts about one family unit.
2. INTERPRETER—Someone who describes history through various mediums such as programs,
    costumed characters, or lectures.
4. PEDIGREECHART—A chart outlining the ancestors of an individual.
6. ANCESTORS—A person from whom one is descended.
8. SOCIALHISTORY—The study of the everyday lives of ordinary people.
9. PATERNAL—Related through the father's line.
10. TRADITION—The handing down of statements, beliefs, legends, customs, information, etc., from
    generation to generation, especially by word of mouth or by practice.

Lesson 8 Home Sources Word Search

```
+ + S + N Y + H + + + B + I +
+ + + D L E O + + + G I + N +
+ + + I R M W + + E + B + T +
+ + M + E O + S N + + L + E +
+ A + + + C E P + + E + R +
F + + + + A E + A + + + M +
Y R A T I L I M R + P + E E +
P H O T O G R A P H S E C N +
V + + G C A R D S + + + R T +
+ I Y + + + + + + + + U S +
+ + T + + + + + + + + + O + +
+ + + A + + + + + + + + S + +
+ + + + L + + + + + + + + + +
+ + + + + + + + + + + + + + +
+ + + + + + + + + + S S A M +
```

Over, Down, Direction

BIBLE(12,1,S)   CARDS(5,9,E)
FAMILY(1,6,NE)   GENEALOGY(11,2,SW)
HOME(8,1,SW)   INTERMENT(14,1,S)
MASS(14,15,W)   MILITARY(8,7,W)
NEWSPAPERS(5,1,SE)   PHOTOGRAPHS(1,8,E)
RECORDS(9,7,NW)   SOURCE(13,12,N)
VITAL(1,9,SE)

```
+ + + + + + Y + Y + + + + Y +
+ + + + A R + G + + + C R +
+ + + + O I O + + + + E A +
O + + T F L L + + + + M N +
+ B S + A A H I D D E N E O L
+ I I E + + M + B + + + T I A
H + N T A R T I F A C T E T C
+ E + + U + Y R L + R B R C I
G + + + + A E R + Y + O Y I D
+ + + + + C R + L + + O M D E
+ + + + O + + Y D E + K + E M
L A N R U O J I + + W S + + M
+ + D + + + A + + + + E + + +
+ S + + + R + + + + + + J + +
+ + + + Y + + + + + + + + + +
```

```
Over,Down,Direction
```

```
ARTIFACT(5,7,E)            BOOKS(12,8,S)
CEMETERY(13,2,S)           DIARY(9,11,SW)
DICTIONARY(14,10,N)            FAMILY(5,4,SE)
GENEALOGY(1,9,NE)              HIDDEN(7,5,E)
HISTORY(1,7,NE)            JEWELRY(13,14,NW)
JOURNAL(7,12,W)            MEDICAL(15,11,N)
MEMORABILIA(15,12,NW)      OBITUARY(1,4,SE)
RECORDS(8,8,SW)
```

Crossword Lessons 6 – 12

Across

5.   PRIMARYSOURCE —A piece of evidence from the past that was created during the event.

6.   FACT —Something that actually exists; truth; reality.

7.   HIDDENSOURCE —A source of information you might not automatically think of when you search for family records.

10.   MEMORABILIA —Items collected and kept because of personal or historical significance.

13.   INTERMENT —Location where a person is buried.

14.   SOURCE —People, documents, artifacts, and print or digital materials.

15. HOMESOURCE —Document or clue found in your home.

Down

1. BURIALFILE —A file created on a military man or woman who dies while in service.
2. PROOF —Evidence or argument establishing or helping to establish a fact or truth of a statement.
3. SECONDARYSOURCE —Sources created after an event by people who do not have firsthand knowledge of the event.
4. HISTORICALCONTEXT —Placing a person in the time period in which they lived.
8. OBITUARY —Notice of someone's death in the newspaper.
9. CITATION —Bibliographic origin of evidence.
11. ARTIFACTS —Memorabilia passed down through the generations.
12. EVIDENCE —Something that pertains to an issue in question.

Crossword Lessons 13 – 15

Across

2. ENUMERATION —A numbered list of data.
4. CENSUS —An official count of a population which records specific details about individuals and families.
5. DEATHCERTIFICATE —An official document issued when a person dies.
6. MARRIAGELICENSE —An official document issued to a couple so they may be married.
7. VITALRECORDS —Governmental records on life events such as birth certificates, marriage licenses and death certificates.

Down

1. ENUMERATIONDISTRICT —A geographic region defined as a tract, area, or district, in which a census is taken.
3. BIRTHCERTIFICATE —An official document issued when a person is born.

Cause of Death Word Search

```
S C + + + + + C + + Y + + + + + + + + L + + S E
+ I O + + A + + H + X + + + + + + + O + + E H D
+ + S L + + L + O E A R G A D O P + C + + P + E E
+ + + O I + + O L + + + + + + + K + + T + + A M
+ + + + R C + P E + + + + + + + J + + I + + + T A
+ + + + + E O + R B + + + + + A + + C + + + + S +
N Y F + S P L + A + U + + + W + + I + + + + T +
O + R A A H + C + + + R + + + + M + + + + + R S
I + + E T + I + S + + + + + + I + + + + + O I
T + + + T T + N + O + + + + A + + + + + + + K S
P + + + + N Y + G + I + + S A I R E H T P I D E O
M + + + + + E L + L + R I J A U N D I C E A + + R
U + + + + + + S I + E T E T Y P H U S + G + + + H
S + + + + + + + Y V I S + T + + + + + U + + + + P
N + + + + + + + D E + + + R + + + E + + + Y + E
O + + + + + + R + + R + + + A + + + + + V + + N
C + + + + + A + + + + + + + + + + + R + + +
+ + + + + + C + + + + + + + + + + + U + + + +
+ + + + + O + + + + + + + + + + C + + + + +
+ + + + Y W I N T E R F E V E R Y S + + + + + +
+ + + M + + + + + + + + + + + S + + + + + + +
+ + + + + + + + + + + + + + + N + + + + + + +
+ + + + + + + + + + + + + + + I + + + + + + +
+ + + + + + + + + + + + + + + U + + + + + + +
+ + + + + + + + + + + + + + + Q + + + + + + +
```

Over,Down,Direction)

AGUE(22,12,SW)	LOCKJAW(21,1,SW)
APOPLEXY(5,8,NE)	MYOCARDITIS(4,21,NE)
ARTERIOSCLEROSIS(16,16,NW)	NEPHROSIS(25,16,N)
CHOLERA(9,1,S)	PODAGRA(17,3,W)
COLIC(2,1,SE)	QUINSY(17,25,N)
CONSUMPTION(1,17,N)	RUBEOLA(12,8,NW)
DIPTHERIA(23,11,W)	SCURVY(18,20,NE)
DYSENTERY(10,15,NW)	SEPTICIMIA(24,1,SW)
EDEMA(25,1,S)	SHINGLES(5,7,SE)
FATTYLIVER(3,7,SE)	TYPHUS(14,13,E)
HEATSTROKE(24,2,S)	WINTERFEVER(6,20,E)
JAUNDICE(14,12,E)	

Occupation Crossword

```
H N A M G A B R + A + R R C N J R T R +
+ T + + + H E + P + O E A + A O E I E S
+ + I + D F O P + T W R + R M Y K N V M
+ R + M F R R O A O N + E + H N R K E I
R + O U S E A G F I + P + A C E A E B T
+ E L T N D I G F E P + A C T R P R + H
N B K T A V E E O I R N L C A M A W E R
+ A I R A R X R D O L A D O W + + + + +
+ C M N A + E S + A N M E M F A R M E R
E + + L + B H M G + + O R P P + + + + +
A + + + I R + G U + + W M T L + + + + +
+ E + + I O E + + N + S A A O + + + + R
R + R E C R E M + + + E D N N W + + + O T
+ E V O N A C L U V + A + T M + + T O R
+ E L + N + C O L L I E R + A + S P + E
+ + + A + A + + + + + H + + N A M + + T
+ + + + B + U + + + + + + + P A + + + N
+ + + + + Z I T H E R I S T N + + + + A
+ H T I M S N W O R B N A M S D A O L C
S A W Y E R + + + + + + + + + + + + + +
```

(Over,Down,Direction)

ACCOMPTANT(14,5,S)
AERONAUT(1,11,SE)
ALDERMAN(13,6,S)
APPRENTICE(10,1,SW)
BAGMAN(7,1,W)
BALER(5,17,NW)
BARKER(6,10,NW)
BEVER(19,5,N)
BLUFFER(2,7,NE)
BROWNSMITH(11,19,W)
CANTER(20,19,N)
CARNIFEX(14,1,SW)
COLLIER(7,15,E)
DIPPER(9,8,NE)
DRAGOON(5,3,SE)
ENUMERATOR(11,13,NW)
FARMER(15,9,E)
FOWER(9,5,NE)

HEADSWOMAN(12,16,N)
HOOFER(6,2,SE)
JOYNER(16,1,S)
LAGGER(11,8,SW)
LOADSMAN(19,19,W)
MAWER(16,7,E)
MERCER(8,13,W)
NAVIGATOR(4,9,NE)
OILMAN(6,12,NW)
PARKER(17,6,N)
PASTOR(15,17,NE)
PLOWMAN(15,10,S)
REDSMITH(8,8,NW)
SAWYER(1,20,E)
SHRIEVE(8,9,SW)
SMITH(20,2,S)
TINKER(18,1,S)
TOPMAN(20,13,SW)

VULCAN(10,14,W)   ZITHERIST(6,18,E)
WATCHMAN(15,8,N)

1. How many immigrants passed through Ellis Island?

    12 million

2. Who was the first immigrant to arrive on Ellis Island when it reopened in 1900?

    Annie Moore

3. As immigrants ascended the stairs to the great hall, how many different chalk marks could a doctor use to identify an illness or issue with an immigrant?

    17

4. View the medical chart on Stop 3: The Great Hall. What did the chalk marks identify? Name them.

Suspected mental defect	Definite signs of mental illness	
Back	Conjunctivitis	
Trachoma	Eyes	Face
Feet	Goiter	Heart
Hernia	Lameness	Neck
Phisical & lungs	Pregnancy	Scalp (Fungal)
Senility		

5. How long did immigrants remain on Ellis Island?

    Days, weeks, and sometimes months

6. Explain the literacy test.

    After 1917, immigrants over the age of 16 were presented with passages from a Bible which they were to read. If an immigrant failed the literacy test they could be deported.

7. In 1909, how much money was an immigrant required to have before they were allowed to enter the United States?

    $20.00

8. What two places did the ferry boats take processed immigrants?

    New Jersey and Manhattan

`.
ac

Vocabulary Review Lessons 21-30

```
+ + + + + + + + + + + + + + + + + Y E
P + + + + + + + + + + + + H + S R N
N A T U R A L I Z A T I O N P + H S O I
+ + S + E + H G M + + T + A + I + C T L
+ N + S + P R C + M N + R + P + + R I E
+ + O + E A H + R E I G + M + + + A S M
+ + A I V N + E M A O G A + C + + P O I
+ + U E T + G U M T E N R E + + + B P T
S + T + + A C E O E I S M A + + + O E +
T + O + + O R H R F R E E + N + + O R +
A + B + D + P G E L T A + R + T + K + +
B + I + + + S I E I Y R A U T I B O +
L + O + + + T + R M + S C L I P P I N G
E + G + + + + Y + + M + T + + + + + + +
+ + R + + + + + + + I + + + + + + + +
+ + A T O M B S T O N E + + + + + + + +
+ + P N A L P H C R A E S E R + + + + +
+ + H + + + + + + + + + + + + + + + +
+ + Y + + + + + + + + + + + + + + + +
+ + + + + + + + + + + + + + + + + + +
```

(Over,Down,Direction)
AUTOBIOGRAPHY(3,7,S)
CEMETERY(15,7,SW)
CLIPPING(13,13,E)
DOCUMENT(5,11,NE)
EPHEMERA(5,4,SE)
GRAVE(8,4,SW)
IMMIGRANT(8,3,SE)
IMMIGRATION(12,15,NW)
NATURALIZATION(1,3,E)
OBITUARY(19,12,W)
PASSENGERLIST(1,2,SE)
PHOTOGRAPH(7,11,NE)
REPOSITORY(19,10,N)
RESEARCH(14,11,NW)
RESEARCHPLAN(15,17,W)
SCRAPBOOK(18,3,S)
SHIPMANIFEST(18,2,SW)
STABLE(1,9,S)

211
© 2018 Jennifer Holik World War II Research & Writing Center

```
TIMELINE(20,8,N)
TOMBSTONE(4,16,E)
```

About the Author

Jennifer Holik is an acclaimed author, researcher, and educator, dedicated to uncovering WWII history by piecing together biographical stories of soldiers' lives that have never been told before.

She has a rare talent for telling WWII stories in an emotive way: lending a 'new voice' to this period of history by shedding light on a soldier's relationships with their loved ones, family and friends. In portraying the human side of warfare she reveals in a poignant, heartfelt, original way what it was really like to have a son, brother, best friend or spouse go off to fight this incredulous war and risk making the ultimate sacrifice for liberty and freedom. Through the research and stories, Jennifer provides healing of the past for clients and those who have already left us.

Based in Chicago, Illinois and Amstelveen, Netherlands, her unique talent and capacities bringing to life a soldier's story by new research techniques provides a rare glimpse into a soldier's personal life. The facts she unravels about his web of relationships provide family members a chance to revisit their soldier's never-told-before story and 'personal war journey' in a new way. In doing so, it allows family members as footsteps researchers, to live their soldiers' pain and glory – memorialize their stories through writing – ultimately, serving as a tribute to their sacrifice; and a testament to our great country.

Learn more at The World War II Research and Writing Center http://wwiirwc.com

Contact the author at info@wwiirwc.com

About the Cover Designer

Sarah Sucansky is a freelance graphic designer / art director living near Minneapolis, MN.

About the Contributor

Terri O'Connell is travel professional who has been involved with genealogy since 1999. A short unexpected illness claimed the life of her grandfather and left her with many unanswered questions about his family. Through the years, she has had many great discoveries in this family and her other lines as well. Relating travel to genealogy is second nature, we all want to see where our ancestors came from and experience a part of their life.

You may find more about Terri, her genealogy research and travel business through the following websites:
O'Connell Travel   http://www.oconnelltravel.com
Finding Our Ancestors   http://www.findingourancestors.com

…nifer Holik

…ing the Answers Through WWII Travel

Finding the Answers: Researching World War II Army Service Part 1

Finding the Answers: Researching World War II Army Service Part 2

Finding the Answers in the Individual Deceased Personnel File

Finding the Answers: Discovering World War II Service Online

Finding the Answers: Researching Women in World War II

Finding the Answers: Starting World War II Research

Faces of War Researching Your Adopted Soldier

Stories from the World War II Battlefield
World War II Writing Prompts

Stories from the World War II Battlefield Volume 3
Writing the Stories of War

Stories from the World War II Battlefield Volume 2
Navigating the Service Records for the Navy, Coast Guard, Marine Corps, and Merchant Marines

Stories from the World War II Battlefield Volume 1
Reconstructing Army, Air Corps, and National Guard Service

Stories from the Battlefield:
A Beginning Guide to World War II Research

The Tiger's Widow

Stories of the Lost

Engaging the Next Generation: A Guide for Genealogy Societies and Libraries

Branching Out: Genealogy for Adults

Branching Out: Genealogy for High School Students

Branching Out: Genealogy for 4th-8th Grades Students

Branching Out: Genealogy for 1st-3rd Grade Students

To Soar with the Tigers